CÆSAR'S ARMY

CÆSAR.

From a Colossal Bust in the Museum at Naples.

CÆSAR'S ARMY;

A STUDY OF THE

MILITARY ART OF THE ROMANS IN THE LAST DAYS OF THE REPUBLIC.

BY

HARRY PRATT JUDSON.

BIBLO and TANNEN

New York

Biblo & Tannen Booksellers and Publishers, Inc.
63 Fourth Ave.   New York 3, N. Y.

Library of Congress Catalog Card Number: 61-12877

Printed in the U.S.A.

Noble Offset Printers, Inc.
New York 3, N.Y.

PREFACE.

————•◦•————

THIS little book is an attempt to reconstruct Cæsar's Army so as to give a clear idea of its composition and evolutions. It is hoped that students of Cæsar's writings and students of military science alike may find interest in such a study.

The Commentaries of Cæsar are the story of his wars. They are military history. It is true that they were intended largely for civilian readers at Rome. Still, they imply throughout a certain amount of military knowledge that all Roman citizens were supposed to have. The modern student can hardly be said to read understandingly, unless the text conveys to his mind the same idea that it conveyed to the intelligent Roman reader to whom Cæsar addressed it. Hence it seems clear that we should at least seek to gain those notions of the military art with which the Roman reader was familiar, and in the light of which Cæsar described his campaigns.

Many of these facts are entirely lost. Many others we can reach at best only approximately. Our inferences, based sometimes on meagre data, may often be erroneous. And yet is it not better to have even such an inadequate idea than no idea at all?

It is needless to say that in these pages the work of modern scholars has been laid heavily under contribution. Especially the exhaustive and ingenious treatise of Rüstow has been followed in many particulars. It has been the aim of the author to reach the truth, and to present it as clearly as he could, giving credit where the investigations of others have been of use, and never hesitating to set forth different conclusions where the circumstances seem to warrant.

War is barbarism. But the story of man has no epoch in which war has not existed. The history of war is the history of the development of the human. mind. The military science of each age is almost the exact reflex of the civilization of that age. And no study of the achievements of man can be complete unless we understand the method of the hostile collision of nations.

The history of military science is yet to be written. Thus far, only some fragments exist. This work is intended as an essay at grouping and illustrating some such fragments.

THE UNIVERSITY OF MINNESOTA,
MINNEAPOLIS, February, 1888.

CONTENTS.

————•◆•————

I.

II.

III.

IV.

VII.

LIST OF ILLUSTRATIONS.

———•◦•———

ABBREVIATIONS.

---◆◇◆---

A. = *Caesar de Bello Africano.*
App. = Appian.
B. G. = *Caesar de Bello Gallico.*
C. = *Caesar de Bello Civili.*
Dio. = Dion Cassius.
G. = Göler, Caesars Gallischer Krieg, Tübingen, 1880.
Gen. = Albericus Gentilis, De Armis Romanis.
Gro. = Grotefend, Zur Romischen Legions geschichte.
H. = *Caesar de Bello Hispanico.*
Jal = Jal, La Flotte de César.
Jung = Jung, Leben und Sitten der Römer in der Kaiserzeit.
K. = Krohl, De Legionibus Reipublicae Romanae.
Lange = Lange, Mutationum Historia.
L. = Lindenschmidt, Die Alterthümer unser heidnischer Vorzeit.
M. = Marquardt-Mommsen, Handbuch der Röm. Alterthümer, Bd. 5, 1884
N. = Nissen, Das Templum.
N. = Histoire de Jules César, par Napoléon III.
Notes = Notes to Allen and Greenough's New Cæsar.
P. = Polybius.
Plut. Cæs. = Plutarch's Cæsar.
Plut. Pomp. = Plutarch's Pompey.
R. = Rüstow, Heerwesen und Kriegführung Cäsars.
R. K. = Rüstow and Köchly, Geschichte des Griechischen Kriegwesens.
Ro. = Robertson, History of Charles V.
Sch. A. = Schambach, Die Artillerie bei Cäsar.
Sch. R. = Schambach, Die Reiterei bei Cäsar.
Schef. = Scheffer, De Militia Navali Veterum, 1654.
Suet. = Suetonius.
T.·G. = Tacitus, *De Germania.*
U. = Upton's United States Army Infantry Tactics, 1883.
V. = Vegetius.

CÆSAR'S ARMY.

———o·o;ʘ;oo———

I. THE ORGANIZATION.

1. THE INFANTRY OF THE LEGION.

§ 1. The chief strength of the Roman army was the legionary infantry. The cavalry was merely auxiliary to this in field operations and was comparatively weak in number. The engines (corresponding to our artillery) were used in siege operations, but very little in the field. The heavy infantry furnished by the allies (*auxilia*), though generally organized and trained after the Roman model, were rather used to make a show of force than for much important service in battle.

B.G. III, 25

The European armies of the middle ages were composed almost wholly of cavalry; the individual horseman being encased in heavy armor and equipped with sword, spear and battle-axe. In modern armies the infantry is again the main arm of the service. Unlike the Roman legions, however, our infantry is greatly strengthened by a powerful field artillery. No army of mere cavalry can be very effective unless in partial and temporary operations.

Ro. I, § II, p. 80, 81.

§ 2. The tactical unit of the Roman infantry was the legion (*legio*). Cæsar had under his command at different times a varying number of legions.

A *tactical unit* may be defined as a body of troops under a single command, by a combination of several of which a higher unit is formed. Thus in the army of the United States, the tactical unit of the army is the *corps;* each corps should contain three *divisions;* each division, three *brigades;* each brigade, four *regiments* (or battalions); each

U. §§ 365, 551, 718, 748.

regiment, ten *companies*. The company is the lowest unit of organization in the United States army.

The organization of European armies is in the main similar to that
of our own country; the main difference being in the size and sub-
division of the regiment.

Each tactical unit has a commanding officer, who receives orders
from the commander of the next higher unit. Thus, the captain of a
company reports for orders to the colonel of his regiment; the colonel,
to his brigade commander (usually a brigadier-general), etc., etc. Each
commanding officer regulates the formation and movements of his command by a combination of the proximate units of which it is composed;
his orders being given to the commanders of those units.

§ 3. The Roman legions were designated by numbers, probably given according to priority in formation. The corps of a modern army are distinguished in like manner.

Cæsar had under his command in Gaul, at different times, the legions
numbered I, III, VII, VIII, IX, X, XI, XII, XIII, XIV, XV.

B.G. I, 7^2.

B.G. I, 40^{13}.
II, 21, 23^1.

B.G. I, 10^3.

When he came to Geneva, in the spring of the year 58 B.C., he
found only one legion stationed in the farther province. This was the
10th (Legio X), afterwards so distinguished for fidelity and courage.
As soon as the Helvetians set out through the territory of the Sequani,
Cæsar hastened to Hither Gaul, enrolled two new legions (XI and
XII),* and called from their winter quarters the three (VII, VIII, and
IX) that were stationed in that province. It was these six legions,
together with auxiliaries (both horse and foot), that composed the army
with which the Helvetians were conquered and Ariovistus was driven
across the Rhine.

B.G. II, 2^1.

In the campaigns of the years 57, 56 and 55 Cæsar had eight legions;
the six used in the previous year, 58, and two of new levies (Legiones
XIII and XIV).

B.G. V, 24^8.
G. 169.

In the year 54, probably in the spring, Cæsar enlisted a new legion
(XV). The 14th was divided. Five of its ten cohorts were scattered,

---

* We learn the numbers from B. G. II, 23. XI and XII are the highest
of those numbers, and hence doubtless belonged to the two new legions.
In the after narrative Cæsar in no case mentions a legion with a number
higher than XII without having previously referred to a legion or legions
newly raised. So we have little difficulty in tracing the numbers of his
legions. The numbers are specifically given by Hirtius in his commentary
(commonly called Bk. VIII).

the men being used to fill up the depleted ranks of the other legions. Thus Cæsar had in that year eight and a half legions under arms. Of these, fifteen cohorts (all of Legion XV and five cohorts of Legion XIV) were destroyed with Sabinus.

At the opening of the campaign of 53 B.C., Pompey loaned Cæsar B.G. two legions (I and III). One new one was raised, which received the VI, I, 32⁵. same number (XIV) as the one Cæsar had divided, and of which five G. 205, cohorts were lost with Sabinus. These ten legions were used in the note 3. operations of the year 52.

In the commentary written by Hirtius Pansa (de Bello Gallico, Bk. B.G. VIII, VIII) the legions are repeatedly mentioned by number; although, 2, 4, 6, 8, unfortunately, with considerable confusion where the Mss. agree, and 11, 24, 54. moreover with considerable variation in the Mss. If we should follow B.G. VIII, the text of Pansa, we should find the 12th legion in three different places 2, 24. at the same time: then, too, he mentions a 6th legion, which we no- B.G.VIII, 4. where else find in Cæsar's army. However, by using some care we can G. pp. 333, trace the different legions from place to place pretty accurately. It is 334, 336, 338, clear enough that in his last campaign in Gaul, Cæsar had eleven legions, 340, 343, 353, although Pansa makes no mention of the levy of the additional legion. 354, 363, 369, Very possibly it was numbered XV, as Göler conjectures, to take the 373, 374. place of that Legio XV that had been destroyed with Sabinus in 54 B.C.

For a careful study of the history of Cæsar's legions, see the dissertation of J. G. Krohl, *De Legionibus Reipublicae Romanae.*

§ 4. The officers in command of a legion were originally the military tribunes (*tribuni militum*), six in number. These were appointed partly by the *Comitia* at Rome, partly by the consul, or, frequently, by the proconsul himself; but always from the knights or nobles. The old requirement of military experience had become obsolete in Cæsar's time, so B.G. I, 39 that the tribunes were mostly selected mainly from political considerations. It can readily be seen that this did not add to their efficiency. The six assigned to each legion were divided into three pairs, and each pair took the command for two months. During this period the two alternated on duty day by day. This custom seems an odd survival of the peculiar Roman jealousy of a single command, as in the case of the consuls. Their duties were, a general superintendence of the legion, the nomination and assignment to duty of the centurions, and to preside at courts-martial. They were often detached to obtain supplies, such tribunes being very probably from the four not on duty with the legion. They formed the natural channel for petitions or other communication from the soldiers to the general. They were also summoned to councils of war by the commander of the army. The tribunes, like the staff of a modern infantry regiment, were mounted.

B.G. III, 7³.
B.G. I, 41.
B.G. IV, 23⁵; V, 28².

This constant change in command and variety of duties, together with the merely political source from which most of the tribunes came, made them hardly reliable to lead soldiers in battle, and Cæsar accordingly soon devised a better plan. Without displacing the tribunes, he stationed a *legatus* (§ 30) with each legion — in the first place merely as a witness for the general of the way in which each officer and soldier performed his duty, afterwards as the actual commander of the legion in battle. This important reform of Cæsar remained under the empire ; the legate so assigned being distinguished as *legatus legionis* (§ 29).

B.G.
I, 52; II, 20;
V, 1¹, 25⁴,
47², also
notes, p. 64;
M. V. 457.

Rüstow considers the duties of the tribunes to have been mainly administrative and judicial; *i.e.*, as having to do with an oversight of the rations and equipments of the troops, and with the cognizance of military offences. This is true as far as it goes. Still, we meet repeated instances in which the tribunes undoubtedly commanded in actual battle. Their command of detachments composed of one or more cohorts, is not infrequent. The many duties of the tribunes are divided among a number of officers in a modern army. The *quartermaster* (whether of brigade, regiment, or company) sees to arms, equipments, and clothing. The *commissary* provides food. *Courts-martial* are composed of details from the various officers. Thus the whole administration of the army is systematized and made more effective.

R. 12.
B.G. II, 26;
V, 52; VII,
47, 52, 62.
B.G. VI, 39.

§ 5. The normal or full strength of a legion in Cæsar's time we have no adequate means of learning. This is to be regretted, as a knowledge of the fact in question would help us to comprehend the Roman tactics. However, the effective strength in the field we can estimate with tolerable accuracy. From the experience of modern armies we know that the number of effectives ready for duty in the field always falls considerably below the number on the rolls ; and again, that even the number on the rolls rarely approximates very closely to the full strength of any organization as prescribed by the tactics. And we may be very sure that in like manner the effective strength of any legion must have varied constantly with the exigencies of the campaign — always, however, or nearly always, being less than that of a full legion just recruited.

In his account of the battle of Pharsalia, Cæsar speaks especially of the great depletion some of his legions had suffered. In that battle his legions had an average strength of C. III, 88, 2750 men. Those of Pompey averaged a little over 4000. 89. Rüstow estimates the average effective force of the legions R. p. 3. throughout Cæsar's campaigns at from 3000 to 3600 men. Göler puts the normal strength at about 4800, besides 300 G. p. 213. *antesignani* (§ 36). These estimates cannot be far from the truth.

Cæsar in one place speaks of a detachment of two legions of infantry B.G. V, 49 and a few cavalry as hardly 7000 strong. That would make about 3500 to the legion.

In the return from Britain in B.C. 55, two transports came to land B.G. IV, 36 below the main port, and the soldiers debarked and marched overland. 37. From these two ships 300 soldiers landed. Assuming the two transports to have been of about the same size, that would average 150 men to a ship. Now Cæsar had 80 transports and an unknown number of B.G. IV, galleys. He lost 12 vessels in the storm. It seems likely that those 12 22³, 31³. were transports, as they lay at anchor, and hence would be more exposed to the storm than the galleys, which were hauled up on the beach. Then at that rate the 68 transports remaining carried 10,200 men. B.G. notes, Allowing for staff officers and servants, the two legions must have P. 135. averaged somewhat less than 5000 men. At the outbreak of the civil war, Cæsar had with him at Ariminium only the XIII Legion (C. I, 7). But Plutarch (*Cæs.* 32) says that Cæsar had at that time 5000 men.

So we may fairly assume that that number was in round numbers the strength of a legion when its ranks were full.

Gellius, 16; 4, 6.

§ **6.** The legion was divided into ten cohorts (*cohortes*) ; each cohort into three maniples (*manipuli*) ; each maniple into two centuries (*centuriae, ordines*).

The *tactical unit* of the legion was the cohort; of the cohort, the maniple.

C. I, 64; III, 91.

The half of the maniple Cæsar usually calls *ordo*. The term *centuria* occurs only twice in the Commentaries; and it is at least doubtful in each case whether reference is made to the divisions of the maniple at all. We should notice that the word *ordo* is also used in other senses than the above. It often means a rank, or line, of soldiers; often a relation of rank among officers, as *primorum ordinum centuriones*, sometimes it refers to the officers themselves; and frequently it denotes a mere position in the array.

The maniple, as the tactical unit of the cohort, consisted from day to day of the same men, so far as these were present. Each time the maniple was formed, it was divided, presumably according to the height of the soldiers, into two equal parts. These were the *ordines*. Thus it will be seen that these did *not* necessarily consist from day to day of the same men; as, of course, if any should be absent, the division would not be made at the same point in the line on successive days. The *ordo* corresponded exactly to the *platoon* of an American company. The maniple corresponded to our *company*.

§ **7.** With Göler's estimate of 4800 men to the legion, each cohort would contain 480 men ; and each maniple, 160 men. Rüstow's computations are based on an average strength in the field of 3600 in the legion. That would give 360 to the cohort, and 120 to the maniple.

§ **8.** Each maniple was under the command of two centurions (*centuriones*), one (the senior in rank) in charge of the first *ordo* ; the other (the junior), in charge of the second *ordo*. Each centurion probably had a subcenturion (*optio*) to assist him. The *optio* was chosen from the ranks by the centurion. The centurion, like the line officers of our

Varro; Festus; Paulus Diac.

infantry, was on foot. As a badge of his office, he carried a short staff (*vitis*), or baton; this was in token of his power of inflicting punishment.

§ 9. Of the six centurions in a cohort, the senior centu- M. V, rion of the first maniple was called *pilus prior;* the junior, 368-374 *pilus posterior.* The senior of the second maniple was *princeps prior*, and the junior was *princeps posterior.* The senior of the third maniple was *hastatus prior*, and the junior, *hastatus posterior.*

Thus the terms *pilus, princeps, hastatus* referred to the first, second, and third maniple respectively. This is plainly a survival of the old organization, in which the soldiers of the first line were called *pilani* (*pili*), those of the second *principes*, and those of the third *hastati* (or *triarii*). Such distinction was entirely lost as applied to the soldiers, in the new organization of the legion by cohorts. The only traces of it we find in the three maniples whose union formed a cohort, and in the titles of the centurions of those maniples.

We readily learn the *ordo* the centurion commanded by the epithet *prior* for the first and *posterior* for the second.

The cohort to which a centurion belonged was indicated by its number in the legion; *e.g.*, the lowest centurion in a legion was *decimus hastatus posterior; tertius hastatus prior* would refer to the centurion in command of the first *ordo* of the third maniple of the third cohort; and the senior centurion of the whole legion was *primus pilus prior*, or simply *primipilus.*

§ 10. The senior centurion of a maniple must have com- M. V, manded the maniple. Each cohort was under the command 371-72. of its *pilus prior;* and the *primipilus*, at least in time of battle, practically directed the legion.

Such an arrangement would hardly be feasible in a modern army. Only the solidity and uniformity of the Roman array made it possible for them.

§ **11.** The position and duties of a centurion corresponded very nearly with those of non-commissioned officers in a modern army. They were chosen from the ranks, as are our sergeants and corporals, and were very rarely promoted to the grade of tribune. However, their responsibilities (not their rank) were in some respects (§ 10) like those of our commissioned officers. The centurions were usually nominated by the tribunes. They received their appointment, however, from the commanding general.

§ **12.** The relative rank of the centurions in a cohort is not difficult to learn, and there is little doubt that it was as explained in the sections just preceding. The order of their rank throughout the legion, however, — or, in other words, the rank of the centurions of any one cohort relatively to those of any other, — is quite a different matter. We have no clear and positive information on the subject, and the various theories formed are based on isolated references, and on inferences from the general spirit of the Roman organization and from the probable course that human nature, as we know it, would take under conditions like those in which the Romans were.

The main facts with which any theory must accord, are the following : —

1. The centurions were plainly divided into *classes* according to rank. There is constant reference to those of the first class (*primorum ordinum*). Cæsar in one place speaks of a

centurion who for especial gallantry was promoted from the eighth class (*ab octavis ordinibus*) to the position of *primipilus*, senior centurion of the first cohort (§ 9).

2. We may infer from this last reference (*ab octavis ordinibus*) that there were *at least eight* classes. Of course there may have been more.

3. From an expression of Tacitus (Hist. III, 22 : *occisi sex primorum ordinum centuriones*) we infer that at that

time there were *at least six* centurions of the first class. As the time to which he refers was that of the emperor Galba, not much more than a century after Julius Cæsar, it seems likely that no material change had been made meanwhile.

4. A passage in Vegetius (II, 21) gives us some idea of the order of promotion. We quote : —

Nam quasi in orbem quemdam per diversas scholas milites promoventur, ita ut ex prima cohorte ad gradum quempiam promotus vadat ad decimam cohortem ; et rursus ab ea, crescentibus stipendiis, cum majore gradu per alias recurrit ad primam.

5. The centurions of the first class (*primorum ordinum*) held so high rank that they were regularly invited to the council of war, in company with the *tribuni militum* and *legati*.

B.G. V, 28², VI, 7⁶.

On these and a few minor facts, ingenious military antiquarians have constructed very elaborate and very diverse theories. The most prominent of these theories, with a few considerations both for and against them, are as follows : —

Rüstow conjectures that the centurions of each cohort form one class. There would then be ten classes in the legion, with six in each class. The regular order of promotion would be, through all the six grades of the tenth cohort, then from the sixth through to the first place in the ninth cohort; and in like manner until every grade had been passed to that of *primipilus*. According to this view, the *centuriones primorum ordinum* were those of the first cohort, six in number.

R. pp. 8-11.

It will be seen that this scheme accords with 2 and 3 above. The passage in Vegetius (4 above), Rüstow gives this interpretation : As vacancies occurred in the ranks of any cohort, they were filled by detailing men from the next lower cohort. Thus recruits would always fall to the tenth cohort, and the first would contain the very flower of the legion. Hence, under ordinary circumstances, when it became necessary to appoint a centurion, selection would be made from the privates of the first cohort (presumably from its first maniple), and he would be assigned as a centurion (*hastatus posterior*) of the tenth cohort (*decimus*). Then he would pass successively through the grades of that cohort, then through the grades of the ninth, and so on, until he became first centurion of the first cohort. Thus the circle (*orbem*) or service would be complete.*

G. pp.
222–28.
Göler devises a different scheme. In the first place, to the 60 centurions of the legion he adds 60 subcenturions (*optiones*), making a total of 120. The subcenturions he calls simply centurions, just as in our army a lieutenant-colonel is commonly called merely " colonel," or a brigadier-general is usually addressed as " general." Then he makes 12 classes of rank, each class comprising 10 centuriones ; *i.e.*, one from each cohort. The first class (*centuriones primorum ordinum*) would include the 10 *pili priores*, or, in other words, the commanders of the 10 cohorts. The second class would be the 10 *pili posteriores;* and so on through the 6 classes of real centurions, the sixth being the 10 *hastati posteriores*. The seventh class he considers to have been the 10 subcenturions of the *pili priores;* and in like o der to the twelfth class, the 10 subcenturions of the *hastati posteriores*.

It will at once appear that this theory also accords with the essential points, 3 and 4, above. Göler would explain Vegetius in this way : —

When a private soldier was promoted, he became subcenturion to the *decimus hastatus posterior*. As he rose in rank, he passed from cohort to cohort, but always as subcenturion to the *hastatus posterior*, until he reached that position in the first cohort. His next step in promotion would lead him from the *twelfth* to the *eleventh* class, and he would return to the tenth cohort as subcenturion of the *decimus hastatus prior*. Thus again and again he would complete the circle (*orbem*), going through the cohorts 6 times in the 6 classes of subcenturions, and 6 times in the 6 classes of centurions, until at last he would reach the rank of *primipilus*. Here his promotion usually ended.

Rüstow argues that the *cohorts*, as well as the centurions, were carefully distinguished in rank; that it is well known that the earlier Roman custom of beginning the battle with less experienced troops, and reserving the veterans for an emergency, had by the time of Cæsar been quite reversed; so that the first line of the legion (the first four cohorts) must have included the choice soldiers; and hence that the centurions would in all probability have been graded in like manner.

M. p. 371.
Marquardt objects to the scheme of Rüstow, that thereby promotion would make the commander of a cohort merely a subordinate in the next higher cohort, an arrangement quite impossible to the military mind. Moreover, as Göler says, the most experienced and skilled offi-

---

* This is an amplification of the interpretation of Vegetius by Rüstow; but merely carries out the suggestions of the latter.

cers would be grouped in the first cohort, and the least experienced and skilled would be gathered in the tenth — an arrangement obviously unpractical.

Rüstow remarks, however, and the remark is not without weight, that there was not, after all, a very great difference between the different cohorts of a legion in point of soldiership; nor again a very wide distinction in the same regard between the centurions and the privates. The Roman organization was marked by a peculiar solidarity, very much unlike our own; and while, of course, the officers had great influence on the fortunes of the battle, yet that influence must have B.G. II, 20[2] been very considerably less than in a modern army.

But the strongest point in favor of some such plan as that of Göler is the fact that the *primi ordines* are sometimes mentioned in such a way as to imply that they held immediate relations with all the cohorts in the legion. Thus, after the council of war that preceded the opera- B.G. I, 41[2]. tions against Ariovistus, the legions that had been panic-stricken arranged *with the tribunes and centurions of the first class* to make their apologies to Cæsar. This would imply that the *primi ordines,* like the tribunes, were immediately accessible by all the soldiers. It would be difficult to imagine the troops of the other nine cohorts coming for such a service to the officers of the first. Certainly it would seem more natural for the men of each cohort to go to their own commander. Passages of similar import are quoted by Marquardt from Livy, Hyginus, Tacitus M. p. 371. (II, 89), Frontinus, and others. The scheme of Marquardt, it may be noted, is the same as Göler's, without the subcenturions. This would make but six classes, and cannot be reconciled with point 2 above.

The principal objection to the system proposed by Göler is the fact that subcenturions seem not to have been in the grades of promotion, but were more probably chosen from the ranks, each by his own centurion (§ 8). If we take away these, we are at once reduced to the six classes of Marquardt, and meet the same difficulty.

One striking difference between the Roman organization and that of modern armies is in the matter of the number of officers. The Romans had far fewer than we. In neither cohort nor maniple do we find any trace of officers corresponding to the commissioned officers in one of our companies, or even to our relatively numerous corporals. The centurions seemed to have all the functions that we should assign to sergeants. They must, besides that, have exercised at least a portion of the duties of general supervision and command that belong to a captain and lieutenants of our infantry. Each *prior centurion* must have had some such general authority over his maniple; and each *pilus prior*, besides the direction of his maniple, must have had some charge of the cohort. For the command of the legion, as we have seen, the Roman methods provided.

The objection of Marquardt to Rüstow's scheme of rank applies with equal force both to Marquardt's own plan and to Göler's, as well as to Rüstow's. According to the scheme of either of the two former, a centurion who had commanded maniples, *e.g.*, *primus hastatus prior*, on promotion would become second in command of a maniple, *e.g.*, *decimus princeps posterior*. This would be quite as little according to modern military ideas as to promote the commander of a cohort to a subordinate place in another cohort. Then to make the two theories named quite consistent, we should make the first three classes contain the *priores*, in the order of *pili*, *principes*, and *hastati*; and the second three classes should comprise the *posteriores*, in the same order.

This, however, would provide for but *six* classes, and we see that there must have been not less than *eight* (2, above). If we adopt the view of Göler, and add six classes of sub-centurions to the six of centurions, we at once run counter to a strong probability that subcenturions (*optiones*) were not in the regular line of promotion, but were chosen each by his own centurion. At least, this seems to have been the fact both before and after the time of Cæsar; and hence very likely was not different at that time. A fair verdict on each of the ingenious theories thus far propounded would perhaps be, "not proven."

Livy;
Varro;
Festus;
Paulus
Diac.

2. THE STANDARDS.

§ **13.** Each legion had as its standard an eagle (*aquila*, C. III, 64.
Fig. 1), usually of bronze or silver, on a wooden staff. This

was entrusted to the care of the
first cohort, and usually to its
senior centurion (*primipilus*).
Hence this officer was sometimes
called *aquilifer;* though the same
term was applied to the men he
selected to carry the standard
(Fig. 4).

Each cohort, also, had a stand- B.G. II, 25
ard of its own (*signum*, Fig. 2).
The bearer of this was called
signifer. Sometimes the legion

Fig. 1. for brevity was called *aquila*, and H. 30.

in like manner the cohort was denoted by *signum*. The *signum* H. 18.
was usually an animal — a sheep, for instance — on a staff.
Of course it would differ for different cohorts, so that the men
in the confusion of battle might know their proper place. B.G. IV, 26[1]

The cavalry and light
troops (§§ 17, 18) car-
ried a *vexillum* (Fig. 3).
This was a little banner,
white or red, attached to
a short horizontal piece
of wood or metal sur-
mounting the staff.

Fig. 2. There was another

Fig. 3.

banner called *vexillum*, the standard of the general. This B.G. II, 20[1]
was white, with an inscription in red letters giving the name C. III, 89.
of the general, his army, etc. It was placed near the gen- Dio Cassius
eral's tent in the camp, and when displayed was the sign for Lib. 40.
march or battle.

Fig. 4. *Aquilifer.*

In the period when the maniple was the tactical unit of the legion, each maniple had its *signum*. Göler thinks this to have been the case even in Cæsar's army. But a consideration of the account of the battle with the Nervii would lead to a different conclusion. Cæsar relates that of the fourth cohort all the centurions had fallen, the standard bearer had been slain and the standard lost. This certainly seems to imply that the cohort had only one standard and one standard-bearer.

Again, in speaking of the flight of the servants on one occasion when a foraging party was suddenly attacked, Cæsar says *se in signa manipulosque coniciunt.* We interpret, *the servants threw themselves among*

G. pp.
239–40.

B.G. II, 25².

M. p. 439.

B.G. VI,
40¹, also
notes, p. 163.

the cohorts and maniples. That is, they rushed for safety into the intervals between the cohorts (*in signa*), and also even into the smaller intervals between the maniples (*in manipulos*). Here *signa* seems to refer to the cohorts.

3. THE MUSIC.

§ 14. The musical instruments used in the Roman army were the bugle (*buccina*, Fig. 5), the trumpet (*tuba*, Fig. 6), the cavalry trumpet (*lituus*, Fig. 7), and the horn (*cornu*). This last was made of the horn of a buffalo, and provided with a silver mouthpiece. The others were probably of brass.

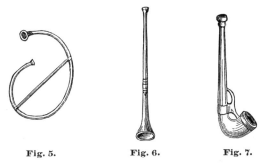

Fig. 5.   **Fig. 6.**   **Fig. 7.**

Cæsar mentions as musicians only *buccinatores* and *tubi-* cines. The former seem to have used the *cornu* as well as the *buccina*.

B.G. II, 20[1] VII, 47[2]. C. II, 35.

The Romans knew very well a fact familiar to modern tactics, that, to carry a command amid the tumult of battle or down a long line of march, the penetrating notes of a brazen horn are much more effective than the sound of the human voice. And accordingly the signals for the various evolutions of march and battle were given by horn and trumpet, first by the horn, at command of the general, then taken up by the trumpets. The bugle seems to have sounded the divisions of the day — reveille, noon, and night-fall.

We know that there were more trumpets than horns.
Quite likely each maniple had its trumpeter, and each cohort
its *buccinator*.

4. THE BAGGAGE TRAIN.

C. I, 81.
B.G. V, 1².

§ **15.** The heavy baggage of the legion (*impedimenta*)
was carried by pack-animals (*jumenta, jumenta sarcinaria*),
either horses or mules.   Wagons or carts, while occasionally
used by the army, were generally found only with the sutlers

A. 75.

(*mercatores*) who followed the legions.   The personal baggage (*sarcinae*) was carried by the soldiers (§§ 45-48).

R. pp. 16-19.

§ **16.** Rüstow has made elaborate calculations of the quantity of baggage a legion must have had.   We follow his
estimates in the main, making such adaptations as may be
warranted by deviation from his figures for the size of the
legion.

We may reckon the load of one pack-animal at 200 lbs.
The first thing would be the tents (*tentoria, tabernacula*).
These as described by Hyginus were on a square base, 10
feet on a side, with a wedge roof.   Ten men could use such

Hy. 1.

a tent.   Hyginus estimates 8 men in a tent.   Yet he allows
one to every 10 men, as one-fifth of each *contubernium*
should always be on guard duty; and hence of the 10
belonging to any one tent, only 8 would ever occupy it at
the same time.   It seems safe to consider that the *contubernium,* a group of soldiers messing together in a tent, was 10
in number also in Cæsar's army.   Then, each centurion had
one tent.   So a maniple would need 14 tents for the centurions and a strength of 120 men.   Allowing two for the servants, the entire number would be 16.   That would make
48 for a cohort, and 480 for a legion.   To this number
must be added those needed by the six tribunes and their
servants, or perhaps 12 more.   If tents are allowed also for
subcenturions, perhaps we should estimate 60 or 30 more,

according as two subcenturions or one should be allowed to one tent.

The tents were of leather (*pelles*). The weight of one, including two upright poles, one ridge-pole, and a supply of pegs, must have been at least 40 lbs. One horse, then, could carry five such tents. It seems more likely, however, that we should estimate one pack-animal to each tent; *i.e.*, one to each centurion and one to each *contubernium*. In this way would be carried provisions for a week, with hand-mills (§ 47), blankets, etc. [B.G. III, 29²; R. 47.]

For pitching camp there must have been needed a full supply of stakes, tools, etc. As these were for general use, they could not have been divided among the pack-animals of the cohorts. So we may add one animal to each cohort for this service. Thus the cohorts would have at least 49 beasts. To each beast should be allowed one servant (*calo*), who could attend to a centurion or *contubernium*, and on the march would lead the animal conveying the baggage under his charge. [B.G. II, 24²; VI, 36³.]

The higher officers had, besides at least two riding-horses each, a still greater number of pack-animals. We shall not be far astray if we assign to each tribune three pack-animals and five servants. Thus the number of the pack-horses or mules in the baggage train of a legion reaches at least 520. [B.G. VII, 65⁵.]

If we consider the normal strength of one of Cæsar's legions to have 4800 men, the maniple would have had 160. This excess of 40 men over the estimate above would have required four tents and other appurtenances, and four pack-animals to carry them. That would add 120 animals and the same number of servants to the baggage train, giving a total of 640 beasts of burden. However, even if this is the nearly correct number for a normal legion, we must remember that a legion very rarely had its normal force. Rüstow's estimate of 520 animals cannot be far out of the way as the baggage train of one of Cæsar's legions in the field. [G. p. 213.]

5. THE AUXILIARY INFANTRY.

§ **17.** The auxiliaries (*auxiliares*) were raised from subject or allied states by enlistment, by conscription, and by treaty. Of course in no case were they Roman citizens.

Among the auxiliaries obtained by voluntary enlistment were the light-armed troops (*milites levis armaturae*, Fig. 8),

Fig. 8.

a. Slinger. — *b.* Light-armed soldier. — *c.* Legionary on the march. — *d.* Legionary ready for battle. — *e.* Light-armed soldier.

used for skirmishing or rapid movements for which the heavily loaded legionaries were hardly adapted (§ 46). Then there were the slingers (*funditores*, Fig. 8), casters of stones and leaden balls, those from the Balearic Islands being especially skilful; and the archers (*sagittarii*), often from Crete or Numidia.

B.G. II, 7¹, 10¹.

Of the organization of the auxiliaries conscripted or supplied by the allies, little is known definitely. We may infer that it would depend much upon the nation; but in case of long service the Roman general doubtless gave some attention to their improvement. They were for the most part used to make a show of strength, thus impressing the enemy with fear, or to aid in constructing fortifications, or similar work. Cæsar never placed much dependence on them for actual battle. As they were usually posted on the wings of the army, they were often called *alarii*.

B.G. I, 51
III, 25.

The light-armed auxiliaries (Fig. 8) wore a short jerkin, or jacket, of leather, without the corselet; and they carried a light, round shield (*parma*) instead of the heavy *scutum*. The archers had neither corselet, helmet, nor shield, as their bow and quiver would prevent their carrying them. Their arms were protected by very thick sleeves.

6. THE CAVALRY.

§ **18.** Originally in the Roman army a body of cavalry, about 300 strong, of Roman citizens, was attached to each

Fig. 9.

legion. This custom had been discontinued by Cæsar's time, although afterwards it was revived under the empire. Cæsar's cavalry consisted entirely of auxiliary troops, raised in like manner and from the same sources as the auxiliary infantry; and these were massed in a single body. During the Gallic war the cavalry attached to the Roman army

B.G. I, 15;
V, 5.

averaged about 4000 in number. When the legions were in winter quarters, the cavalry contingents were scattered to their homes. There were, however, a few enlisted men in this arm of the service who remained constantly under the standards. They were Gauls, Germans, and Spaniards. (Fig. 9.)

B.G. V, 46³; VII, 13¹; V, 26²; VII, 55¹.

The organization of the auxiliary cavalry contingents was after the manner of their nation; modified more or less, doubtless, by Roman customs. Contingents of from 200 to 400 men were commanded by *praefecti equitum*. A larger body was always under a Roman commander.

B.G. IV, 11⁴. B.G. I, 52⁵.

Of course the enlisted cavalry was organized entirely in the Roman way. A tactical unit was the *ala*, or regiment, 300 to 400 strong, commanded by a *praefectus equitum*. The *ala* was divided into *turmae*, squadrons, of perhaps 33 men each, including the commander, the *decurio*. The *turma* was divided into three *decuriae* of 11 men each.

A. 29, 78. B.G. VI, 84. A. 29. G. p. 229.

7. THE ARTILLERY.

§ 19. For battles in the open field the Romans of Cæsar's day seldom used anything corresponding to modern artillery. In defending and attacking fortified places, however, engines of various kinds were employed for hurling missiles, and, in case of attacking, for battering down walls. As such engines could not easily be improvised, and must always be at hand in a campaign involving siege operations, it seems quite likely that a siege train would usually be carried with the army. That would involve a body of men who should see to its transportation and who should understand setting it up, using, and repairing it. Possibly a detachment of the *fabri* (§ 36) was entrusted with this work.

R. pp. 16-19.

§ 20. Of the exact construction of the Roman artillery of this period we have no precise accounts. We can only infer what it was from the names applied, from its use, and from what we know of Greek military engines and of those in general use at a later time.

§ **21.** The missile weapon Cæsar almost universally calls *tormentum.* This word (from *torquere*, to twist) plainly refers to the source of power, viz., the elasticity of *torsion.*

§ **22.** There seems no reasonable doubt that the Greek and Roman artillery of the same age had about the same construction ; and, further, that there had been no material change in that construction at Cæsar's time for some two or more centuries. Then we shall be quite near the truth if we examine the Greek artillery of a somewhat earlier day than Cæsar's.

M. 518.

M. 523.

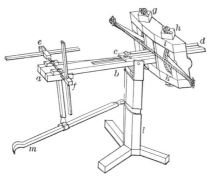

Fig. 10. *Catapult.*

§ **23.** The heavy missile weapons were of two kinds : those for hurling their missile in a direction horizontal, or nearly so, and those that threw a heavy mass at a considerable angle. The former shot large arrows, and were called catapults (*catapultae*). The latter kind usually cast heavy stones, but were sometimes provided with blocks of wood. They were called *ballistae.*

R.K. pp. 378 seqq.

§ 24. Catapult and ballista alike had three essential parts : the standard, a track for the missile, and the arrangement that provided motive force.

The standard (*l*, Figs. 10, 11) was made strong and heavy, so that the machine might rest firmly on the ground and be unshaken by use.

The track for the missile (*ab*, Figs. 10, 11) was a stout

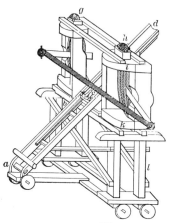

Fig. 11. *Ballista.*

framework in which fitted a slide (*cd*) which slipped smoothly up or down the track. The missile was placed in a groove on the upper side of the slide. By a system of levers the track of the catapult could be aimed to direct the missile at a greater or less vertical angle. By a similar arrangement a variation in the horizontal aim could be made.

The apparatus for providing force consisted in the first place of a framework of three compartments, formed by two horizontal bars or sets of bars (*k*, *i*) and four uprights. Through the middle compartment extended the missile track (*cd*). The other two compartments were fitted alike. A block (*h*, *g*) bored with a vertical hole was placed over a similar hole in the upper part (*i*) of the framework. Strands of hair were passed from below, through the holes in the frame and block, over an iron cross-pin, and back down through the holes again. The other end of these strands was passed in like manner around a corresponding cross-pin on the under side of the framework. The strands were then stretched to their utmost tension (the cross-pins meanwhile being twisted in opposite directions) and the blocks on upper and under side screwed fast.✻ There was thus formed a strongly twisted rope or cluster of ropes. ✻A rigid bar of wood or metal was then inserted through each cluster. These bars rested in beds cut in the two outer uprights. The inner end of each bar rested against the front of the corresponding inner upright. The outer ends of the bars were then connected to each other by a strong cord (a bowstring).

It will at once be seen that when the bowstring is drawn back, the bars are drawn from the beds ; and that when the bowstring is let go, the torsion of the ropes at once throws the bars violently back against the beds again, thus tautening the bowstring and propelling the missile along the track.

In using the *tormentum* the slide was pushed forward until its hinder end was at the bowstring. This was then slippèd under a trigger-like arrangement near the end of the slide, where it was held fast. Through a ring in the rear of the slide was tied a rope, which then passed around a windlass. By means of this windlass the slide was drawn back, pulling the bowstring with it. The missile was then laid in the groove of the slide, and, the trigger being raised, the bowstring was released, and drove the missile towards its destination.

§ 25. The weight of a heavy catapult has been estimated, R.K. pp. 38 according to size, at from 84 lbs. to 600 lbs. seqq.

At least two men would be required to manage the smallest. Of course each increase in the size of the weapon would demand more men.

From a statement of Philo, we can estimate the cost of a Philo, p. 62 rather small catapult of his day, allowing for change in the purchasing power of money, at about $200.

The distance to which a missile could be cast was not more than 1200 ft.

A. 31. *a.* The *scorpio* (Fig. 12) was a small catapult capable of being managed by one man. It consisted of a firm framework, on which was fastened a bow of steel. This was bent by a windlass, and shot its arrow (18 in. long) to a distance of some 300 to 400 ft.

Fig. 12. *Scorpio.*

§ **26.** The weight of the ballista was considerably greater than that of the catapult. At least six men would be required to manage the smallest.

The cost of course would depend on size. A ballista throwing a weight of 10 minæ (9 lbs.) perhaps cost $1600 in Philo's time.

The range of the ballista was about the same as that of the catapult.

§ **27.** The weight of the ancient artillery was considerably greater in proportion than that of modern times. A mortar throwing a bomb of 120–130 lbs. weighs about 40 lbs. A ballista which threw a stone of 135 lbs. weighed about 200 lbs. ; *i.e.*, five times as much as the mortar.

This circumstance would of itself account for the fact that the Greeks and Romans made much less use of field artillery than do modern armies. Then, too, the clumsy construction of catapult and ballista made them much more difficult to transport than a modern field battery.

Another objection to their employment in the field was the long time required to make them ready.

§ **28.** The main use of artillery, then, was to defend a for- Sch. 5. tified town or camp. In almost every fortified town of the Greeks or Romans, they were kept in considerable numbers ; and when needed for siege operations were obtained from such towns. The walls of a camp were often defended by what we might call light artillery, catapults of small caliber B.G. II, 8. and scorpions.

In attacking fortifications the ballista was used to break down the battlements, the catapult to sweep the wall of defenders and thus protect the column of assault or the workmen busied with the *agger* or the battering-rams.

Ships of war were often provided with artillery, some- B.G. III, 14 times placed on towers. These were used, not merely against IV, 25. a hostile fleet, but often against an enemy on the land.

There seems no doubt that artillery was conveyed with B.G. II, 8; Cæsar's army in the field. Rüstow's statement to the con- C. 51, 56; trary is certainly erroneous. Quite likely a certain amount A. 31, 77; was assigned to each legion ; though of this we have no cer- Al. 9. R. p. 26. tain evidence. Whenever the army took a position of defence, B.G. VIII, the artillery, posted behind the legionaries, played a promi- 14. nent part.* *The walls of the camp were often lined with B.G. II, 8; VII, 41, 81. *catapultae* and *ballistae.* *

In the time of Vegetius (probably at the close of the fourth century C. 51, 56. A.D.) each legion was provided with 55 *carroballistae* and 10 *onagri.* The *carroballista* was a small catapult, and the *onager* a light *ballista.* The *onager* (wild ass) was so called from the story that that animal in fleeing from its enemies cast stones against them with its hind heels. In the Austrian army, to-day, 112 pieces of artillery are attached to an army corps of about 50,000 men. Other nations employ about the same ratio.

---

* From this same passage (B. G. VIII, 14) we must infer that Cæsar took artillery from the camp and used it in the field.

8. THE STAFF AND STAFF TROOPS.

§ 29. The general staff of an army consisted of the commanding general, the legates, the quæstors, the assistants, the guards, and the engineers (*fabri*).

§ 30. The legates (*legati*) were men of senatorial rank, who were assigned to the proconsul in greater or less numbers by the senate. In military service they were the lieutenants of the commanding general, and were by him often placed at the head of detachments of one or more legions, with varying powers. But all their powers were derived from the general. Cæsar made a great improvement in organization by placing a legate regularly in command of each legion. Such legate was afterwards known, under the empire, as *legatus legionis*, by way of distinction from a legate with greater powers.

B.G. I, 52.
M. p. 457.

§ 31. The quæstor, assigned by lot to superintend the finances of a province, also had charge of the supplies of the army. In the execution of this duty he saw to the food, pay, clothing, arms, equipments, and shelter of the troops. To do all this, he must have had under him a numerous body of men. He filled the place both of adjutant-general and of quartermaster-general in a modern army.

§ 32. There always followed the general a number of young men as his attendants (*contubernales, comites praetorii*), who were volunteers, and who aimed to learn the art of war. They composed the nobler part of the *cohors praetoria*, or attendants of the general.

Many of them could be used as aids in the administrative department of the army, or on the field of battle. When they were very numerous, they were formed into detachments, or sometimes joined the body-guard, and could thus directly take part in battle.

§ **33.** The inferior part of the *cohors praetoria* was composed of *apparitores*, lictors, scribes, and servants. There were also included the *speculatores*, or spies.

The *speculatores* were men selected for obtaining news and carrying despatches. They preceded a marching column, and also accompanied the flanks, at a considerable distance, so that no surprise or ambuscade might be met. There were usually ten to each legion. Of course the commanding general had an indefinite number at his disposal. M. p. 547. B.G. II, 11

§ **34.** By the *body-guard* we must understand, not choice legions, especially honored by the commander, as was the Tenth by Cæsar, but troops which constantly stood in a near relation to the general. In Cæsar's army these were, in the first place, mercenary troops, possibly small bodies of German cavalry, which he used as a personal escort; and, in the second place, the *evocati*. B.G. VII, 13.

§ **35.** The *evocati* were those who had completed their term of service and still remained with the army; or even having returned to their homes, had resumed their place in the ranks at the solicitation of their old commander. Such men, centurions and privates, must have been of priceless value to a general who aimed at sovereignty, as did Cæsar. They must have exerted much more influence on the mass of the army than could higher officers. They were on the same plane in every way as the common men, and so would more easily lead them to their own way of thinking. C. III, 91.

The *evocati* in Cæsar's army were formed into a regular organization, divided into centuries. They enjoyed special privileges. Although footmen, they had not only pack-animals, but riding-horses as well, and used them on the march. They could thus also be employed by the general as orderlies, to carry commands, or as scouts. In battle the *evocati* were formed near the general, for the protection of B.G. VII, 65.

his person. In their ranks were those of the *voluntarii* who were not otherwise employed, and who could have no better school in which to learn the art of war. These veterans, composing the flower of the whole army, were ready to give examples of courage to all.

§ **36.** The engineers (*fabri*), at whose head was the *praefectus fabrum*, or chief of engineers, must have belonged to the staff. They were employed in building bridges, constructing winter quarters, and very likely in repairing weapons. We must notice that the main Roman weapon, the *pilum*, was useless after it was hurled; but when the victory was gained, the *pila* could be collected from the field, and no great skill or apparatus was needed to make them effective again.

G. V, 11.   It must be noted that *fabri* were often called from the ranks of the legions. Very likely men expert for the duty immediately at hand were thus detailed, and, when the duty was completed, returned to their places in the ranks. Sch. 9.   Schambach thinks that the artillery was managed by details from the infantry, as was done in the main in modern armies so late even as the middle of the eighteenth century. In that case it is clear that the men detailed must have been of sufficient intelligence and mechanical skill not merely to use the *tormenta*, but also to see to their repair.

§ .37. There is some doubt as to the composition of the *antesignani*. Göler thinks that the term applies merely to the four cohorts that formed the first line.

It is Rüstow's opinion that they were a detachment separate from the cohorts. Each maniple possibly had one *contubernium*, or ten men, of *antesignani*, chosen for their experience and efficiency. When needed they could move out from their cohorts in front of the legion, and act as light troops, or skirmishers. They would be more valuable and steady for such service than the auxiliaries, and could form a valuable support for cavalry. On the march they were always without heavy baggage (*expediti*). This service furnished abundant advantages for training subalterns ; and Cæsar himself regarded the body as a school C. I, 57. for centurions.

II. THE LEGIONARY.

§ 38. The main strength of a Roman army was in the legionary infantry. Of these, naturally, then, we have the most satisfactory accounts. About the auxiliary troops, cavalry and infantry, we have already spoken (§§ 17, 18). Of the legionary, we must now speak more in detail.

1. ENLISTMENT.

§ 39. In the earlier days of the republic the army was a compulsory levy of all the able-bodied male citizens of suitable age. None but Roman citizens were admitted to the legion. All Roman citizens must serve. At the close of the campaign the troops were disbanded, and returned to their homes and their usual avocations. Thus the army was a body of *citizen soldiers,* or *militia.*

But with the great increase in the number of citizens, especially after the social war, only a part were needed for military duty ; and at the same time a plenty were found who were willing to enter the service, led by hope of gain and glory. So the armies became less and less a levy of citizen soldiery, and more and more a body of mercenary volunteers. From this fact certain results speedily appeared. As the Roman army grew to be a disciplined organization of professional soldiers, it became all the more effective ; and the men were the more readily attached to their chosen leader. Meanwhile the peaceful citizens who remained at home, to a great degree lost that military spirit and knowledge which had always before characterized the Roman people. Thus the way was paved rapidly and surely for the coming of a military despotism.

The Legionary.

NOTE. — The *pilum* and *braccae* belong to the time of the empire.

To face page 30.

§ **40.** The enlistment of barbarians in the legions of Cæsar, however, was altogether exceptional. We do read of one legion, the Alauda, which was wholly composed of barbarians. Yet it is undoubtedly substantially true that Cæsar's legionaries were enrolled from Roman citizens, and spoke the Latin tongue.

§ **41.** The second condition of enlistment in the legions was that of age. This we know in the early centuries of Rome was from 17 to 46. In all probability these were the limits in the time of Cæsar. In the army of the United States, in the time of war, the age of the recruit must be between 18 and 45.

§ **42.** In the third place, those only would be enlisted who had sound bodily health, and were of suitable size. What the limit of height was in the Roman army we do not know. In our infantry no one is received whose height is less than 5 ft. 4 in., or more than 5 ft. 10 in. From the fact that the legionary fought with sword and spear, instead of with the breech-loading rifle of modern wars, we may infer that he must have been more muscular and agile than is now necessary; but we cannot infer that he was of unusual size. On the contrary, there is little doubt that the soldiers who conquered the world for Cæsar were as a rule rather under-sized. The historians always emphasized the bigness of the Germans; and Cæsar expressly mentions the small stature of his troops. The Romans had learned the lesson of civilization, that victories in war are gained, not by huge bones and big bodies, but by the trained skill of scientific organization and tactics. Any one of the German giants might perhaps have been more than a match for any individual of his puny Italian enemies; but the barbarian mob of Ariovistus was shattered when hurled against the spears of the legions.

T.G. I, 4.
B.G. I, 39;
II, 30.

2. CLOTHING.

§ 43. All the soldiers of the legion were clothed, armed, and equipped alike (Legionary p. 30, and Fig. 8). Next the skin was worn a sleeveless woollen shirt (*tunica*). Over this was a leathern coat strengthened by bands of metal across the breast and back and over the shoulders (*lorica*). The troops in Trajan's column are represented with tight-fitting trowsers (*braccae*) extending below the knee. It seems likely, however, that these did not come into use among the Romans until after Cæsar's time. Strips of cloth were quite probably worn wound around the thighs (*feminalia*) and around the shins (*cruralia*). The feet were protected by sandals (*calcei*), or by strong shoes not unlike those worn at the present time. Then, in cold or wet weather, the person was covered by the military cloak (*sagum*), a sort of woollen blanket. Of course this was laid aside in battle.

3. ARMOR.

§ 44. The defensive armor consisted of helmet, greaves, and shield.

a. The helmet of the legionary (The Legionary, p. 30) was either of iron (*cassis*), or of leather or cork strengthened with brass (*galea*). That of the officer was distinguished by a plume of red or black feathers (*crista*).

b. The greaves (*ocreae*) were of bronze. They were used to protect the leg below the knee, and were held in place sometimes by straps, sometimes by their own stiffness. Usually but one was worn, on the right leg, as this was the one advanced in the fight.

c. The shield (*scutum*, Fig. 13) was of wood, covered with leather or with iron plates. In the centre was a boss (*umbo*), which was merely a knob designed to strengthen and bind all together. The shield was about 4 ft. long and 2 ft. wide. Often it was curved so as partially to encircle the body. On the outside was painted the badge of the cohort — a wreath or a winged thunder-bolt, for instance. On the inside was the name of the soldier, with the number of the cohort and century, or maniple ; perhaps also the number of the legion. For protection from dust, rain, and the like, during the march the shield was kept in a leathern case.

Fig. 13.

4. ARMS.

§ 45. The offensive weapons were the sword and spear.

a. The sword (*gladius Hispanicus*, Fig. 14) had a blade about 2 ft. long, and several inches wide. It was two-edged and pointed, being thus adapted either for cutting or thrusting. The latter, however, was its customary use. What fearful wounds could be inflicted with this weapon we may see from Livy, 30, 34.

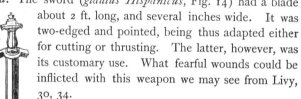

It hung seldom from a body belt, generally from a shoulder belt (*balteus*). This passed over the left shoulder. Thus the sword was on the right side, this being more convenient, since the shield

Fig. 14. was carried in the left hand. As the higher offi-cers had no shields, they wore their swords on the left side, and a dagger (*pugio*) at the right.

b. The spear (*pilum*, Fig. 15) was the characteristic weapon of the legionary. We have no exact account of it as it was in tne time of Cæsar. From the way in which he mentions its use, however, we may infer that it did not materially differ from the pilum of days not very remote from his, and of which we can form some tolerably definite idea.

P. VI, 23.

The pilum of the time of Polybius had usually a square wooden shaft, 4½ ft. long and 2½ in. thick. On one side was a groove extending half the length of the shaft, to receive the iron. This latter was also 4½ ft. long. One half, square in shape, was fitted into the groove, and held in place by two iron nails. The other half, of pyramidal form, projected from the wood and was sharpened at the end. At the base of the shaft there was undoubtedly an iron shoe, so that in camp or bivouac the pilum might be thrust into the ground. The length of the entire weapon appears then to have been 6¾ ft., and the weight can hardly have been less than 11 pounds. Rüstow considers this (Fig. 15) to have been essentially the pilum of Cæsar.

The researches of Dr. Lindenschmidt leave little doubt as to the pilum used during the empire (Fig 16). The iron was longer than the shaft, with a distinct head, which produced the effect of barbs. The entire weapon was probably somewhat lighter than that of Polybius. It was much like a modern harpoon.

Polybius says that, besides the heavy javelin, the soldier carried also another lighter one. Cæsar makes no mention of a second pilum, and all the circumstances of its use lead us to think that his legionary

Fig. 15. undoubtedly had but one. This, says Rüstow, was probably the heavy one. It seems quite as likely that when the light spear (designed, of course, to be used first, as it could be cast to a greater distance) was discarded, the heavy one was somewhat reduced in weight, so as to increase its range. This reduction could not have been so great, however, as materially to impair its efficiency.

Fig. 16.

B.G. I, 25.

In the time of Marius, the upper of the two nails which held the iron in place was of wood. When the missile struck, this pin would be apt to break, and the momentum of the shaft would cause the iron to bend, thus making it useless to the enemy. Cæsar makes no mention of the wooden pin, but he often speaks of the bending of the iron

We can hardly infer, as does Rüstow, that the wooden pin was not used in the *pila* of Cæsar. On the contrary, so many other contrivances of the sagacious Marius were retained, and so few years had elapsed from his day when the Gallic wars began, that it seems altogether probable that the *pilum* of Cæsar was quite the same as that of Marius. At any rate, had Cæsar contrived, or even authorized, any material change in this most important weapon, we can hardly doubt that a writer so scrupulous as he in assigning to the conqueror of Gaul his full meed of praise would have been very careful to narrate this instance also of his hero's ingenuity.

The bending of the iron clearly implies that it was comparatively slender and soft. So we may conclude that it was hardened only at the end. Now this bending, accomplished in the *pilum* of Marius by the breaking of the wooden pin, would have resulted in that described by Lindenschmidt, from the extreme slenderness of the iron as compared with the shaft; and this slenderness would have been made possible by the head, which was of sufficient size and hardness not to be affected itself by the impact.

The point of bending in the *pilum* of Marius was undoubtedly in the part of the iron which lay in the wood; that of the later *pilum* was as undoubtedly above the shaft.

The history of the *pilum*, as we get glimpses of it from time to time, certainly shows a slow evolution. In the light of this fact, it seems probable that in the time of Marius and Cæsar it held an intermediate position between the heavy and somewhat clumsy spear described by Polybius and the more elegant javelin of the later empire. The shaft was probably round. The iron was in all likelihood fitted in a groove, and not in a socket. Where it entered the wood, the head of the shaft was probably protected. The iron was slender, easily bent, hence hardened only at the end and provided with a head. The weight need not have been more than two or three pounds less than that estimated by Rüstow.

Lindenschmidt objects to this estimate (11 lbs.) that it was too great for comfort in carrying, and for hurling to any distance. The first objection is trivial, that being just about the weight of the modern musket. And the trained muscles of the Roman veteran could have found little difficulty in 'hurling an eleven-pound spear with force to a distance of many feet.

5. BAGGAGE.

§ **46.** Besides his arms and armor, the legionary was accustomed to carry various entrenching tools, such as saws, spades, axes, and baskets ; articles for obtaining and cooking food, as sickles, cords, and cooking vessels ; spare clothing and material for repairing any of the clothes or equipments.

R. p. 14. § **47.** The ration of food for one day weighed probably about 1⅔ lbs.   On short expeditions, the soldier must carry his own provisions.   As many as 17 days' rations, amounting to 28 lbs., are known to have been provided and carried.   The ration was usually in the form of coarse flour, or of unground grain which the soldier must crush for himself.

§ **48.** According as the food was for a longer or shorter time, the weight carried, exclusive of arms or armor, must have reached 30 to 45 lbs.

§ **49.** For the convenient carriage of all this baggage, Marius contrived what were known by his name as "Marius's mules" (*muli Mariani*).   The baggage was packed in bundles (*sarcinae*), and these fastened to the upper end of a pole (*furca*), which was forked at the top.   On the march the legionary carried this pole on his shoulder.   When a temporary halt was made without laying aside the baggage, the lower end of the *furca* was placed on the ground, and the soldier could lean on it to rest.   (Fig. 8.)

6. WORK.

§ **50.** The legionary was not allowed to rust from idleness.   When the day's march was done, he must lay aside baggage and arms, and do his part in fortifying the camp.

Some were detailed to the trench and wall, some to erect the tents, some to prepare food for the various messes. When a long time was spent in camp, even then each hour brought its allotted task. There were the regular tours of guard duty, the ordinary work of keeping the camp clean, and of making ready the meals, and regular drills, including gymnastic exercises, which kept each muscle at its best.

7. PAY.

§ 51. Cæsar fixed the pay of his legionaries at 225 M. p denarii a year (about $45.00). A day laborer in Rome at that time earned three-fourths of a denarius a day ; or, in a year of 300 working days, just as much as a legionary. Thus the soldier was better off than the laborer by merely one thing ; to wit, his shelter.

For food and equipments, so far as they were provided by the state, a deduction from his pay was made. As provision, each man was allowed per month four measures (8.67 litres, or a little less than a peck) of wheat. The measure may be estimated to be worth at the highest three-fourths of a denarius. Thus the amount deducted for food cannot have exceeded 36 denarii per year. However, in the provinces, the food, if not given outright, was reckoned at a very low price ; and the same must have been true of clothing and equipments. Moreover, the soldier in active service always expected an increase to his income from booty, and from the gifts of his general.

§ 52. We have no certain account of the relation borne Dj· by the pay of the soldier to that of the officer. But we read, App. 2, 491 Suet. 38. on occasion of a present to the troops, that the centurion Plut. Cæs. received twice as much as the private, the tribune and the 55· cavalry prefect, four times as much. On another occasion, G. 8, 4. we know that the centurion received ten times as much as the private. The former seems likely to have been the ordinary relation of the pay; especially as we must remember that the centurion stood in rank and duties about midway between a sergeant and the captain of a company in a modern army. In the army of the United States, the private of infantry is paid $13.00 a month; the sergeant $17.00; and a captain receives $1800 a year. All are provided with food, clothing, and shelter. A day laborer in most of our cities can earn about $1.50 a day; about the rate of the private in the army, considering that the laborer has to provide for himself.

8. DISCIPLINE.

§ 53. During the civil wars, the stern discipline of the old Roman armies became much relaxed, and commanders had to resort to all manner of means to hold their armies in order. The transition from a citizen soldiery to a mercenary army, on the other hand, paved the way for a discipline more unrelénting than ever.

Lange, pp. 26 seqq.

But the best means of maintaining order then, as now, lay in constant employment. On the march, the daily fortification of the camp left the soldier little time to think of anything but his duty. On occasion of a longer pause than usual, the camp was to be further fortified and arranged, and guard duty must be performed constantly. The Roman method of war made the personal activity of the man an indispensable condition of success. Hence constant practice in the use of weapons was necessary; and this would quite fill out the time.

A. 71, 72.

Then, too, zeal and courage were rewarded no more by mere crowns of leaves, but by more substantial gifts in good coin. So we see that the Roman general was not confined for his discipline to mere brutality.

When generals endeavored to attach their soldiers to their persons, they had to allow them far more license than mere discipline would warrant. Violence to the conquered, misuse of power towards them, robbery and plunder, were at times allowed. What the Romans regarded as purely *military* crimes, such as mutiny, desertion, cowardice, abuse of authority in the army, were punished severely ; not infrequently the penalty was death.

Suet. Cæs. 67, 69. A. 46, 54. C. III, 74.

In a modern army, comparatively trivial offences, such as drunkenness, for instance, are often punished by detention in the guard-house, and sentence to some disagreeable labor, as cleaning the camp, or the like. Expedients like this must have been used in ancient armies as well.

III. TACTICS OF THE LEGION.

§ 54. The *tactics* of a body of troops consists of their arrangement for battle and their movements in the fight, their order of march, their disposition in camp, and all evolutions in passing from one of these forms to another. The *order of battle* is chiefly important, because all the other formations are made with reference to this: and to understand the order of battle of any organized body of soldiers, we must first of all study the arrangement of the *tactical unit* of that body.

MILITARY TERMS.

§ 55. We must explain a few military terms in common use.

1. *English.*

A *tactical unit* is a body, of a number of which a larger body is composed, and which, in relation to that larger body, is thought of as undivided. The tactical unit of the legion was the cohort; of the cohort, the maniple, etc.

A body of troops is in *line* when the greatest extent of the body is at right angles to the direction in which they are facing (Fig. 18); in *column*, when the greatest extent of the body is in the direction in which they are facing (Fig. 21).

Troops are said to *deploy* when they pass from column to line, *retaining the same facing*. In Figure 20, the cohort is marching in column. If they simply halt and face to the left, they are in line of battle, as in Figure 18. This they have done without deploying.

Alignment is making a line of troops straight.

A soldier is said to *face* when, standing still, he merely turns on his heel (to the right, or left, or entirely about).

Fascines are bundles of brush bound together. They are often used for filling a ditch.

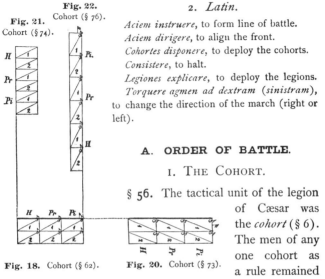

Fig. 21. Cohort (§ 74).

Fig. 22. Cohort (§ 76).

Fig. 18. Cohort (§ 62). **Fig. 20.** Cohort (§ 73).

2. *Latin.*

Aciem instruere, to form line of battle.

Aciem dirigere, to align the front.

Cohortes disponere, to deploy the cohorts.

Consistere, to halt.

Legiones explicare, to deploy the legions.

Torquere agmen ad dextram (sinistram), to change the direction of the march (right or left).

A. ORDER OF BATTLE.

1. THE COHORT.

§ **56.** The tactical unit of the legion of Cæsar was the *cohort* (§ 6). The men of any one cohort as a rule remained together, and all movements of the legion were made by cohorts.

We may estimate the front of a cohort in line of battle at 120 ft.

§ **57.** In all estimates of extent of the legion in battle, march, or camp, we follow Rüstow's figures, which are based on the average field strength of the legion, 3600 men, not on its nominal, or full, strength.

In relating a fight at Ilerda, in Spain, Cæsar states that his troops were drawn up across the top of a ridge, along which the enemy were advancing. He then says that this ridge was just wide enough for *three cohorts in order of battle (tres instructae cohortes,* C. I, 45). The ridge is readily recognized to-day, and measures just about 360 feet across. The circumstances of the fight were such as to leave no doubt that the cohorts were drawn up without any intervals between them; so that this measure gives us the actual front of the cohorts. Thus we get the estimate of 120 ft. for the front of one cohort.

The three maniples of a cohort might have been arrayed side by side, or one behind the other. Rüstow holds to the former arrangement, and Göler to the latter. The reasoning of Rüstow (R. p. 36

seqq.) seems conclusive, in the light of our present knowledge ; and we have adopted the arrangement of the maniples side by side. In that case the two platoons (*centuriae, ordines*) of each maniple doubtless stood one behind the other.

§ **58.** Assuming the three maniples to have been arrayed side by side, this would allow 40 ft. as the front of each maniple. Allowing 4 ft. for the interval between each two maniples, in which intervals the centurions were probably placed, and a corresponding distance of 4 ft. for the centurion on the right of the maniple which formed the right of the line, there would be left 36 ft. front in each maniple for the privates. As each private would require at least 3 ft. of space, the maniple would consist of 12 files (Fig. 17).

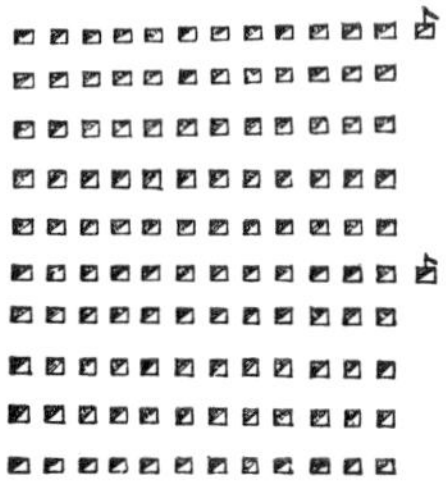

Fig. 17. *Maniple.*

§ **59.** In military language, a *file* is a number of men in a single line, placed one behind another. A number of men in a single line, placed side by side, is called a *rank*.

The interval of four feet between the maniples would be none too much for the centurions. The officer would naturally need more room than a private, as his attention must not only be given to the enemy, but also to his own troops down the line to his left. So it seems likely that the first centurion was at the right of the front rank of the first platoon (*ordo*), and the second centurion at the right of the front rank of the second platoon. Thus the latter officer could keep to their duty the men behind the fighting line, and could see that vacancies ahead should be promptly filled.

§ **60.** The distance from breast to breast, in the file, was probably at least 4 ft. Thus the file was 10 men deep (*i.e.*, there were 10 ranks), and the maniple would form a square of 40 ft. on a side.

In the United States army, the breadth of a man is taken at 22 in., his depth at 12 in.; and there is a distance between ranks, in column of march, of 32 in. from back to breast, or of 44 in. from heel to heel. In line of battle, the distance from back to breast is 22 in., from breast to breast 34 in. (*Upton's U.S. Army Infantry Tactics*, 65, 209).

§ 61. We have assumed that each man in the front rank of the maniple occupied 3 ft. This would be sufficient space to march without being crowded, and to throw the *pilum*. It would not give room, however, for using the sword. Vegetius says that each man needed 6 ft. for that purpose. The men in each rank were numbered, from right to left; and at the command ("*Laxate manipulos*") each B.G. II, 25 odd number stepped forward, thus gaining the desired space.

§ 62. By our estimate, a cohort in line of battle would form a rectangle, 120 ft. front by 40 ft. deep (Fig. 18). The maniple would contain 120 men, and the cohort 360, exclusive of officers.

2. THE LEGION.

§ 63. The order of battle may be offensive or defensive. When arrayed for the first purpose, the legion formed either two lines (*acies duplex*), or three lines (*acies triplex*).

§ 64. In the *acies duplex* there were 5 cohorts in each line.* When the legion was in 3 lines (Fig. 19), 4 cohorts were placed in the first (*acies prima*), and 3 in each of the others (*secunda* and *tertia acies*). Between the cohorts in the first line were intervals equal to about the front of the cohort (120 ft.). Behind these intervals stood the cohorts of the second line. The third line was still further in the

---

* C. I, 83. *Caesaris triplex (acies fuit) ; sed primam aciem quaternae cohortes tenebant, has subsidiariae ternae et rursus aliae totidem suae cujusque legionis subsequebantur ; sagittarii funditoresque media continebantur acie, equitatus latera cingebat.*

rear, and was used as a reserve for the support of the other two. The most experienced and reliable soldiers of the legion were in the four cohorts of the front line.

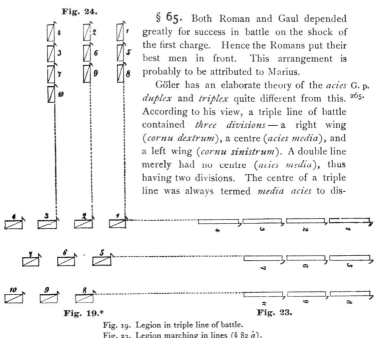

Fig. 24.

§ **65.** Both Roman and Gaul depended greatly for success in battle on the shock of the first charge. Hence the Romans put their best men in front. This arrangement is probably to be attributed to Marius.

Göler has an elaborate theory of the *acies* G. p. *duplex* and *triplex* quite different from this. 265. According to his view, a triple line of battle contained *three divisions* — a right wing (*cornu dextrum*), a centre (*acies media*), and a left wing (*cornu sinistrum*). A double line merely had no centre (*acies media*), thus having two divisions. The centre of a triple line was always termed *media acies* to dis-

Fig. 19.*　　　　　　　　　Fig. 23.

Fig. 19. Legion in triple line of battle.
Fig. 23. Legion marching in lines (§ 82 *a*).
Fig. 24. Legion marching by wings (§ 82 *b*).

tinguish it from the middle line of the cohorts of a legion, *secunda acies*. Each division had a *legatus* in command.

This theory is hardly borne out by the facts. One who reads B.G. I, 49 with care will see that it would be very difficult to reconcile Göler's view with Cæsar's account. Further, in A. 13 we have a *simplex acies* with both right and left wings specifically mentioned; and in B.G. III, 24 a double line (*duplex acies*) has a centre (*media acies*). From these considerations it seems plain enough that Cæsar used the terms *right wing, left wing,* and *centre* quite as they are used of a modern army;

* These diagrams of battle and march are after Rüstow.

applying them in an indefinite way to those parts of a line of battle, but not necessarily implying distinct divisions under separate commanders.

§ **66.** The distance between the lines was probably equal to the front of a cohort (120 ft.). Thus the entire depth of the legion in this order of battle was about 600 ft. The front would extend 840 ft., or, if supported by another legion, 960 ft., including the interval between the legions.

§ **67.** For defensive battle the legion was arranged in one of two ways: in one line (*acies simplex*), or in a circle (*orbis*).

§ **68.** The former was most commonly used to defend the walls of the camp (§ 153). Here a second line was unnecessary; and also considerable depth was needless. Five ranks (the depth of a single *ordo*) would do; one or two, according to the width of the wall, on the rampart, and the rest in reserve at its foot. Allowing 6 ft. (instead of 3 ft.) for each man in the front rank, and arraying the *ordines* side by side, we see that a single cohort would cover 480 ft. of the wall, or a legion 4800 ft., allowing no intervals between the cohorts.

§ **69.** This arrangement in one line without intervals was A. 13 also used in the open field to meet an attempt at outflanking by superior numbers, and also to resist incursions of cavalry or light infantry through the intervals. In this case, however, the cohorts would have their normal front and depth, merely closing the intervals and thus giving the legion a front of 1200 ft.

§ **70.** The circle (*orbis*) was designed for use in the field in case of attack on all sides.

As the circumstances for which this arrangement was intended must have been essentially the same then as now, we may conclude that a cohort would form in a solid square, a smaller division in a solid circle, and a detachment of several cohorts in a hollow square. This latter might have been made circular, to resist attack at the angles. A legion could form the square by placing the first, second, and third cohorts in front, the eighth, ninth, and tenth in the rear, the fifth and sixth in the right, and the fourth and seventh on the left. There would then be a front of 360 ft. and a flank of 320. The inner hollow space would be 280 ft. long and 240 ft. broad, thus making 67,200 sq. ft. This would contain more than 1000 pack-animals.

C. III, 89. § **71.** Under some circumstances we read also of a quadruple line of battle. This was designed to meet a flank attack. Some cohorts were taken from the rear line (*tertia acies*) and placed in line on the right (or left) flank at right angles with the main line of battle.

B. THE ORDER OF MARCH.

The order of march is developed from the battle array. So we must begin with the cohort.

1. THE COHORT.

§ **72.** The line of march (*agmen*) of the cohort was one of two, — *column of maniples* and *column of centuries*.

§ **73.** The column of maniples (*manipulatim*) was formed from order of battle by merely facing to the right (or left). Thus the maniples, it will be seen, were in column (Fig. 20), and the centuries in each maniple were side by side. If the cohort was faced to the right, the order was *pilani, principes, hastati*. As the depth of the cohort in line of battle was 40 ft., of course the column of maniples was 40 ft. wide. But this was a loose order. Allowing 3 ft. to each man, the column could easily have been made only

30 ft. wide. And again, this wide column could have been reduced to half the width by the right (or left) century moving straight on, and the other falling in its rear. Instead of 12 ranks of 10 men, there would be 24 ranks of 5 men. This would make really a *column of centuries by the flank.*

§ 74. The *column of centuries* proper (*centuriatim, ordinatim*) was formed from the order of battle merely by having the maniple on the right (or left) wing of the cohort march straight forward, and the others successively follow. Thus the centuries would be arranged in column (Fig. 21) ; and the order would be *pilani, principes, hastati,* or the reverse, according as the right or left wing moved off first. The width of the column would be the same as the front of a maniple, *i.e.*, 40 ft., including the centurion on the flank.

§ 75. When a cohort marched directly forward, the column of centuries would naturally be adopted. In this order, then, it is likely that Cæsar marched across the Rhine. But we know that he made his bridge *40 ft.* wide. It does not seem at all likely that this distance was that between the piles at the bottom of the river. As the water varied in depth, it could hardly be measured exactly, and different sets of piles quite likely had different distances on the river bottom. On the top, however, an exact distance could have been measured, and must have been preserved. Thus in Cæsar's bridge is another support of our estimate of the front of the maniple.

§ 76. If the march was on a regular road or street less than 40 feet wide, the breadth of the column could easily be reduced from 40 ft. to 20 ft. The right (or left) half of each century would move straight on, and the other half would fall in the rear (Fig. 22). Thus the century would consist of 10 ranks of 6 men each, instead of 5 ranks of 12 men each.

§ **77.** On the march, we should estimate 4 ft. from breast to breast. Then a cohort of 360 men would reach to the following length : —

In column of centuries 120 ft.

In column of centuries, with double number of ranks, 240 ft.

In column of maniples, 144 ft.

In column of maniples, with double number of ranks, 288 ft.

§ **78.** The line of battle (*acies*) was formed from the column of march (*agmen*) as follows : from column of maniples by the commands halt ! front ! (facing to the left, if the original march was to the right ; to the right, if the original march was to the left) ; from column of centuries, the leading maniple would halt, and the others successively march alongside, aligning themselves on the right or left, as the case might be.

§ **79.** We may assume that the usual formation of the column of centuries was with the right in front, *i.e.*, in the order *pilani, principes, hastati*. But we must observe that to form line from this column requires a deploying to the left. Should the enemy be near, this would expose to them the unshielded right side (*latus apertum*). So we may conjecture that, for instance, in a sally from the gate of a camp against a near enemy, the cohort would march with the left in front and deploy towards the right.

2. THE LEGION.

§ **80.** The legion, or a still greater number of cohorts, marched in one of three orders, — in column (*agmen pilatum*) ; in order of battle (*acie instructa*) ; in square (*agmen quadratum*).

§ 81. When the legion is in column, the cohorts march according to their number. If the march is from the right, the first cohort has the lead, then follows the second, and so on. If the march is from the left, the tenth cohort leads, followed by the ninth, etc. Each cohort is in column of centuries.

Between each two cohorts there must have been a small distance. Suppose this to have been 20 ft. Then the length of the legion — the cohorts marching in column of centuries of the usual width — would have been 1400 ft. When the cohorts doubled their number of ranks, the length of the legion was 2600 ft.

For the train of a legion, we estimate 520 pack-animals as the normal strength. In a road 40 ft. wide, 8 animals can easily find room abreast. Then the train would have had 65 ranks. Allowing each rank 10 ft. depth, the train would extend 650 ft. When the road is only 20 ft. wide, the pack-animals would march 4 abreast, and would extend 1300 ft.

Then a legion with its baggage in column of march would extend 2050 or 3900 ft.

§ 82. The march in order of battle is of two kinds, — by *lines* and by *wings*.

a. If the legion marches by *lines*, there are as many columns as there are lines in the formation. Thus in Cæsar's army there would usually be three columns (Fig. 23). In the first column are cohorts 1–4 ; in the second, cohorts 5–7 ; and in the third, cohorts 8–10. Each cohort marches in column of maniples. So by simply facing to the right or left, the legion is again in order of battle.

b. A legion that marches to the front by *wings* forms three columns (Fig. 24). In the first are the cohorts of the right wing, 1, 5, and 8. In the second are the cohorts of the centre, 2, 6, and 9. In the third are the cohorts of the left, 4, 3, 7, and 10. The columns must be as far apart as the distance between their leading cohorts when in line of battle. Each cohort is in column of centuries.

§ 83. The march in square (Fig. 25) was employed for a similar purpose for which the *orbis* was formed. One division of troops, in columns of centuries, leads. Then follows the baggage train, and then a second division of troops in column of centuries. On either wing marches a body in column of maniples. Thus by a simple facing of the wings to the right and left, and deploying of the van and rear, the square is ready to meet the enemy.

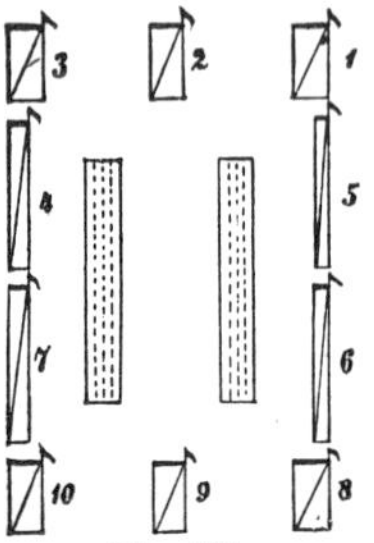

Fig. 25.
Legion in Square.

§ 84. These are conservative estimates. To compare the Roman army with one of modern days, we quote a very comprehensive calculation from the New York *Evening Post*. It must be remembered that an American brigade of four regiments corresponded very nearly with the Roman legion.

"A company of infantry moving in column of fours, the usual marching formation, takes up about 33 yards of depth. A regiment of ten companies will require 330 yards, a company of cavalry about 100 yards, and a battalion of four companies about 450 yards. A six-gun battery of field artillery in column of sections, and accompanied with the usual baggage, requires about 225 yards. From these figures we calculate the length of a column moving on a single road. An infantry brigade of four regiments will take up, exclusive of baggage, 1350 yards. The baggage, including ammunition, will require nine six-mule wagons to each regiment. Each wagon with its team requires 20 yards depth, and for the entire brigade the depth will be over 700 yards. Add this to 1350 yards, and we have nearly 2100 yards, or a mile and a quarter for the depth of the column. If we allow but three regiments to the brigade, we can reduce the depth to about 1,600 yards. For the baggage belonging to different headquarters we must allow a depth of 200 yards.

"Now, coming to a division of infantry, we have but to multiply the foregoing total by the number of brigades in the division. But when we take up an army corps, we have to make calculations for artillery and cavalry, extra baggage and supply trains. Suppose we take as a maximum figure an army corps composed all told of 42,000 men. It has four divisions of infantry, eight to twelve batteries, and at least four regiments of cavalry. Were it able to march close up, on a single road, with all its trains, including reserve supplies, it would stretch out, at the least calculation, about eighteen miles. But it is impossible for a column of this length to keep from stretching, or "lengthening out," as it is technically termed, and so the best authorities make an allowance of 25 per cent, which, added to the 18 miles, makes $22\frac{1}{2}$ miles, or a distance which would take a mounted messenger moving from the head of the column to the rear, if he made good speed and met with no obstruction, at least three hours to make, or moving from the rear to the head, nearly half a day.

"Gen. McClellan, in one of his reports, says: 'If I had marched the entire army, 100,000 men, in one column, instead of on five different roads, the column, with its trains, would have stretched out 50 miles.' In the Franco-Prussian war it was found that a Prussian army corps of 42,512 men, 90 guns, 13,800 horses, and 1300 vehicles took up on a single road 27 miles, 18 miles occupied by the troops and 9 miles by the trains.

"If roads were all broad enough and in good condition, columns could march with a far greater front, and the depth be vastly reduced. But in this country, at least, there are few roads where there is room for a column of greater width than a set of fours to move and leave sufficient space for the unimpeded progress of orderlies and staff officers, or for vehicles which have to go in an opposite direction. It may be asked why the column cannot be kept closed up, why it has to lengthen out? Sometimes a wagon breaks down. It is hauled to one side for repairs and the others pass on. But to haul it to one side consumes some time, mayhap only a few moments, and a few moments again when repaired to re-enter the column. The consequence is a halt of everything in the rear. Neither men nor horses can be marched steadily without a halt and rest every hour, and a halt at the head of the column, or in resuming the march, occasions loss of time to all regiments in rear, which cannot start at once, but must do so successively.

"Again, perhaps, a bridge has to be crossed, and time is lost by the breaking of step, or, perhaps, the change of formation. Perhaps a stream has to be forded, or some obstacle is met in the road. It must be remembered that, in addition to the actual distance accomplished in marching, many other things are required of the soldier. He has to go on guard or picket, he is sent out perhaps as a flanker on the march, or arriving at camp he has to collect fuel and water; more-over, he carries a heavy load, his kit, gun, ammunition, and day's rations, averaging from fifty to sixty pounds. So that perhaps, were we able to calculate all that he has done, we should find he has expended as much strength as would take the ordinary pedestrian over 25 to 30 miles of road."

IV. TACTICS OF THE CAVALRY.

§ 85. The small tactical unit of the Roman cavalry, or of that formed on the Roman plan, was the *turma*, of 32 horses in rank and file. This was probably arranged in 4 ranks of 8 horses. Allowing 5 ft. front room to each horse, the *turma* would have a front of 40 ft., equal to that of the maniple. Taking 10 ft. depth for each rank, the depth of the *turma* would also be 40 ft., again equal to that of the maniple. The order of march could easily be formed from this order of battle.

§ 86. A regiment (*ala*) of 400 horses consisted of 12 *turmae*. The battle array of the cavalry would very likely resemble that of the infantry. It would then consist of several lines, two or three, with intervals between the *turmae*. A regiment of 12 turmae in 2 lines would have 6 in each line ; and the front, including intervals, would be 440 ft. Of course, if it should be desired to overwhelm the enemy with the momentum of the mass of horse, the intervals would be closed up.

§ 87. If the number of cavalry should be considerable, a larger tactical unit would be desirable. Three *turmae*, arrayed side by side, would amount to about 100 horses, with a front of 120 ft., equal to that of a cohort. A regiment (*ala*) of 400 horses would contain 4 such divisions.

§ 88. In attacks in mass, doubtless columns were formed of entire *alae*, perhaps 3 *turmae* front and 4 *turmae* (*i.e.*, 16 ranks) deep. After the success was won, the turmae in the rear could be brought up in the front (*turmatim*) to pursue the scattered foe.

§ **89.** Of course the tactics of the cavalry would depend largely upon their arms, as well as upon their numbers. If provided with missiles, they would doubtless be arrayed in *turmae* only, and would never form columns for attack.

§ **90.** Cavalry were sometimes strengthened by infantry mingled with them. Cæsar used with good effect his *antesignani* for that purpose.

§ **91.** The usual order of march of the *ala* of 400 men was probably in column of *turmae*. If there was room for a column 40 ft. wide, the normal order of battle would be kept by each *turma*. The *ala*, not including the train, would extend 480 ft. The train must have been considerable, and would have added at least a half to the length of the line. A column of 10 *alae*, or 4000 men, which Cæsar sometimes had, would have extended 7200 ft.

§ **92.** If the road allowed the column a breadth of only 20 ft., the *turma* would march with a front of 4 horses and a depth of 8. The *ala* would then need 960 ft., without baggage, and with it 1440 ft. A column of 10 *alae* would require 14,400 ft.

V. TACTICS OF THE ARMY.

A. THE BATTLE.

§ **93.** The core of the Roman army was the legion. Hence we see that in describing the battle array of the legion, we have very nearly explained the mode of battle of the army as a whole.

1. OFFENSIVE.

§ **94.** It is clear that the normal order with the Romans was the offensive. Cæsar usually employed the triple line (*acies triplex*). The legions that composed the line of battle stood side by side, each in three lines.

The third line was designed as a reserve for the other two. The Roman method was to hurl the first line against the enemy. Should this onset not suffice, or should the first line become exhausted, then the second line in turn took up the attack, while the first retired between the intervals and rested. Thus the two lines alternately assailed the foe, until the latter should break. Meanwhile the third line was in reserve. Should the enemy attempt a flank movement, this line was deployed to the left or right to meet it. If no such movement was attempted, or if auxiliaries were at hand to meet it, the third line was held in reserve until the crisis of the battle. Then it was hurled at the enemy in a decisive charge.

Often, also, the third line was busied in fortification, while the first and second covered the work. B.G. I, 25, 52. C. III, 89, 94.

§ **95.** In case a reserve seemed unnecessary, or a greater extension of front was desirable, the legions were formed in

C. I, 83.
two lines (*acies duplex*). On the other hand, circumstances might demand a double reserve, and the legions were then C. III, 89, 93, 94. in four lines (*acies quadruplex*). In this case, the third line was held to support the attack, and the fourth to guard the flanks. For this last service, the fourth line was not behind the third, but was deployed on one side or the other of it — sometimes at right angles to the main line of battle. The fourth line was usually weaker than the other two. Sometimes one flank of the army was in three lines, and the other in four.

§ **96.** We must notice that the Romans placed great dependence on their first charge. And it is significant, in this connection, that the first line was the strongest of the three, and contained the most experienced cohorts.

§ **97.** The cavalry, in an offensive battle, was used for guarding against a flank movement, for taking the enemy in flank, and for hurling upon the enemy when routed, thus to complete his destruction.

B.G. III, 25; VI, 8. C. I, 83; III, 88, 89, 93.
For these purposes, the cavalry was commonly placed on the flanks of the legions. Sometimes it was placed behind the fourth line. Thus the latter could receive an attack of the enemy's cavalry — which being repulsed, the Roman cavalry could issue between the intervals to attack B.G. I, 24, 25. in turn. Often the cavalry was drawn up behind the legions. It was then placed behind the *first* cohorts, as thus they could more easily pass through the intervals for a charge.

C. I, 83; A. 13, 60, 81.
§ **98.** The light troops, archers, and slingers were either placed in the intervals of the cavalry, or thrown out in advance of the legions as skirmishers, or placed on the wings to resist flanking movements. Of course they were of no avail for making a charge.

§ **99.** The front of the line of battle was divided into three parts, the right and left wings (*cornu dextrum, sinistrum*), and the centre (*acies media*). These were often placed under *legati* detailed for the purpose. B.G. I, 52; II, 23. C. III, 67; A. 60, 81.

§ **100.** The most experienced legions were usually placed on the wings; on the wing which was to begin the attack, the best of all. This, again, was in accordance with the Roman custom of trusting much to the impetus of the first onset. C. III, 89; A. 60, 81.

§ **101.** When the line of battle was formed (*acie instructa*), the general passed from legion to legion, addressing each with a brief speech of encouragement (*cohortatio*). He then proceeded to his own post (usually the wing that was to begin the attack). When the right moment arrived, he ordered his trumpeter to give the signal for the onset (*signum*). This signal was taken up by the trumpets of the other legions, and passed down the line. So the attack was made by the legions successively. The cavalry was held in reserve on the flanks, ready to receive flank attacks, and in turn to assail the enemy in the flank. B.G. II, 20 C. III, 90. C. III, 92. A. 82.

The general oversaw the battle, supplied reserves, and was present himself, or sent one of his staff, at every critical point. If victory was won, the cavalry was hurled on the broken enemy to complete the rout; or infantry was advanced to overcome renewed resistance. If the Romans were beaten, the general, with a cloud of cavalry and light troops, covered the retreat to the fortified camp. B.G. VII, 47.

'2. DEFENSIVE.

§ **102.** The fundamental ideas of the Roman defensive were, to make use of ground that would cause as much weariness to the enemy as possible, to delay their approach, to weaken them meanwhile by missiles, and then, at the right moment, to assail them at their weakest point.

§ **103.** Modern armies are much better provided for defensive battle than were the Romans. Our troops are armed with missile weapons which are not useless as soon as used and which are still effective for hand to hand work. The vast improvement in the modern arms of precision is daily making this truth more emphatic. An excellent illustration of a collision between the modern power of resistance and the ancient power of attack is afforded by the battles at Teb and vicinity between the British troops under General Graham and the Arabs of Osman Digma, in 1884. The Arabs, armed with spear and shield, and inspired with frantic courage, rushed in crowds upon the British squares. But the incessant volleys of the repeating rifles poured a ceaseless deluge of balls upon them, and not many of the blacks lived to reach the bayonets. At a few points, where the line was for a moment broken, the lithe Arab with his spear proved a deadly foe ; but rifle and revolver restored the day.

§ **104.** The only missile weapons of the ancients that had any great range, capable of being used in the field, were bow and sling. But the Romans never had many archers and slingers. These were of no use for hand to hand fight, and the legions were of no use for anything else.

§ **105.** Hence great care was exercised in the choice of ground. Whenever it could be done, the army was drawn up where approach was possible only on one side ; and this side difficult on account of a swamp, a watercourse, or some similar natural barrier. If necessary, and time was afforded for the work, approach was further hindered by ditches, *chevaux-de-frize*, pitfalls, or something of the sort.

3. Manner of Attack.

§ **106.** The Roman infantry sought always to gain the advantage of a higher place (*superioris loci*). Their favorite position was on the side of a gently sloping hill, so that the enemy were below them. The enemy had then a disadvantageous place (*locus iniquus*). If at the foot of this hill there was a plain, and the enemy were at a greater distance than the cast of a javelin (10 to 20 paces; *i.e.*, 25 to 50 ft.), then to the enemy was left the initiative. If, however, their adversaries were at the foot of the hill or had set out to climb it, then the Romans rushed against them. B.G. I, 22, 24, 25; II, 8; III, 4; V, 9; VI, 46; VII, 51. C. I, 45, 65, 79; III, 46. B.G. II, 23, 27, 33; V, 49; VI, 40. C. I, 45.

§ **107.** If the distance was considerable, say 250 paces to an enemy just setting out to the attack, or 120 paces to an enemy evidently intending to await the onset, then the cohorts at first moved forward at a walk, probably at an equal pace (*certo gradu*). Having reached the proper distance, they set out at a run (*cursus*), sword in sheath, the first ranks with spears raised in the right hand ready to hurl (*pilis infestis*). At a distance of 10 to 20 paces, the first ranks hurled the spears. This volley at short range threw the enemy into confusion, inflicting numerous fearful wounds. The dead and wounded fell, and thus gaps appeared in the hostile array. Here and there a *pilum* remained sticking in a shield, and thus embarrassed its bearer; or in the thick phalanx two shields were bound together, and so two of the enemy were rendered useless for the fight, unless they let their shields go and exposed their unprotected bodies to the Roman weapons. C. I, 87. B.G. VIII, 9. B.G. VIII, 9. C. II, 92. C. III, 93. B.G. I, 25; II, 23; A. 16

§ **108.** As the spears could be thrown only from a short distance, it is clear that sometimes a rapidly advancing enemy would get near too soon, — the right moment would have passed, — and the Romans must then drop their javelins and engage with the swords. But usually the volley of heavy spears preceded the use of the sword. B.G. I, 52.

B.G. II, 23;
VII, 88; C.
III, 46.
§ **109.** As soon as the first ranks have hurled the spears, they draw their swords and rush forward to take advantage of the confusion and gaps in the enemy's line. The odd numbers of the first rank spring forward to gain room ; the even numbers and the entire second rank follow as a support.

Along the front of the cohort exists now a series of single combats. The third, fourth, and fifth ranks press close up to aid their comrades and to take the places of any who fall, and meanwhile throw their spears over the heads of the combatants among the throng of the enemy behind. The remaining five ranks of the cohort stand fast, as a reserve.

§ **110.** The various acts of the attack are sharply distin- B.G. VI, 45;
C. II, 93. guished in military parlance. Advancing to attack was called *signa inferre*. Then followed the run (*concursus*), then the volley of spears (*emissio pilorum*). If the enemy B.G. I, 25,
52; VI, 8. still held out, there remained the last resort, the onset with the swords (*impetus gladiorum*).

§ **111.** It will be seen that each cohort, if only two ranks hurled the spears at once, could attack five times. At R. pp. 49, 50. Ilerda, each of these attacks consumed at least 20 minutes.

§ **112.** Another advantage sought by the Romans must be noticed. We must remember that their favorite vantage-ground was a hillside, down which they could rush against their enemy. Under such circumstances more than two ranks could hurl the *pila*, and also these weapons would fall B.G. I, 25. with more force.

§ **113.** Of course if the volley of spears was cast too soon, they fell harmless on the ground. It was often quite likely, in the confusion of battle, that such a mistake would be made. Moreover, the Romans were accustomed to throw the weapons while on the run themselves, and against an advancing enemy. Should the latter receive the onset standing, as did Pompey's men at Pharsalia, the volley might C. III, 92. easily be ineffective.

§ 114. Running to the attack gave an impetus that was of great value. But if this run should be begun too soon, there was danger that the men would reach the enemy out of breath and tired, and also that the ranks would be more or less spread apart.

§ 115. It was much in favor of this onset to be made on a hillside down which there was a gentle slope. The momentum thus gained would carry the men against the enemy, whether they would or not. Also, the enemy were more likely to become demoralized at sight of this mass pouring down from above. Moreover, the same circumstance which made the attack heavier, would make it less effective for the enemy to make a charge to meet it.

§ 116. The rush was usually made by a line at once ; or, B.G. I, 52; the cohort on one wing would begin, and the rest of the C. III, 91; A. 82. line would immediately take it up. The second line followed the first at the usual distance (about 200 ft.), and halted as soon as the first became engaged.

§ 117. Should the legions thus attack a continuous line of the enemy, it is clear that they would impinge on that line only at certain places, and there was danger that the enemy would pour into the intervals and attack the cohorts in flank, especially on the right side, unprotected by the shields B.G. I, 25; (*latus apertum*). This could be met by advancing the sec- II, 23; C. I ond line, thus losing the advantage of using this as a reserve ; 44. or, the rear ranks of the first line could be deployed to right and left into the intervals. We find in fact that the second line was generally used as a reserve, through whose intervals the exhausted first line could retire, and behind which it could re-form.

§ 118. How long one line would remain in the fight before it was relieved we have no definite knowledge. But we may easily conjecture that it could hardly have been more than 15 minutes in general. Then the second line would advance to the attack, the first would assemble behind it, re-form, rest, and be ready in turn again to take up the fight.

§ 119. Cæsar usually fought in three lines rather than in two. We may suppose that he brought the third line into action only in case the blows inflicted by the other lines successively proved insufficient to cause the enemy to break. Thus the third line was a last reserve.

§ 120. We see that we must imagine the cohorts in battle as in almost constant motion. The two lines are hurled successively against the enemy, giving the latter no rest, and wearing them out by the incessant blows of the cohorts.

§ 121. When the enemy were finally routed, the cavalry was hurled on the fleeing mass to complete their destruction. Cæsar never failed in this way to follow up a beaten foe. Hence his victories, like Napoleon's for the same reason, seldom proved indecisive.

B. THE MARCH.

§ 122. Every long distance was divided into day's marches (*itinera*). After each two or three days of marching, as a rule, followed a day of rest.*

Each day's march (*iter*) was from one camp to another ; so that " a distance of five camps " means a five days' march.

B.G. VII,
36.

§ 123. The Romans aimed to fight only near their own camp. When they were compelled to break this rule, and

---

* If no such rest was taken, it was regarded as wholly exceptional. See B.G. I, 41, *Septimo die, cum iter non intermitteret*, etc.

fight on the march (*ex itinere*), they usually allowed only a B.G. III, 21, part of their men to engage, the rest being employed in VII, 18. A 18. fortifying.

§ **124.** Vegetius says that the recruits were practised to V. I, 9. march in five summer hours, at the usual pace (*militari gradu*), 40,000 steps (of $2\frac{1}{2}$ ft.), and at quick step 48,000 steps. Five summer hours are equal to about $6\frac{2}{3}$ of our hours. Then in the first case there would be 100, and in the second case 120, steps to the minute. Upton's Tactics, the standard of the United States army, as now revised, prescribes a step of 30 inches, from heel to heel, both in common and quick time, and a cadence of 100 steps per minute for common time and 120 steps for quick time, exactly the Roman standard.

§ **125.** The step (*gradus*) of $2\frac{1}{2}$ (Roman) feet, was the distance from heel to heel, and was one-half a pace (*passus*). This latter was the full distance from the point at which the heel leaves the ground to the point at which the same heel next returns to the ground, and was reckoned at 5 (Roman) feet. It must be remembered that the Roman feet probably was about 0.9708 of an English foot.

§ **126.** The Roman day's march ordinarily covered about R. p. 93. 7 hours, from sunrise (4 to 5 or 6 A.M.) until 11 or 12. Allowing time for rest, it seems hardly likely that they would average more than 30,000 to 40,000 steps in that time. This would be 14.6 to 19.5 English miles.

§ **127.** The average day's march for infantry in the United States army is from 15 to 20 miles (§ 84). Rest is generally allowed at the U. 750. rate of 10 minutes an hour. Taking these facts into account, we see that we cannot be far out of the way in our estimate of the Roman march; especially when we consider what an amount of work had to be performed in fortifying the camp.

Of course forced marches were often made, continuing sometimes even all night.

§ **128.** We must distinguish three forms of march, — the march forward, to the rear, and to either flank.

I. The Advance.

§ **129.** When the column is marching forward, we must distinguish three parts of the army, — the van (*primum agmen*), the main body (*exercitus, omnes copiae, agmen legionum*), and the rear-guard (*agmen novissimum, agmen extremum*).

C. III, 41;
B.G. I, 15.
B.G. II, 19.
B.G. I, 15,
23; II, 26;
C. I, 63, 64.

§ **130.** The van may have one of three objects.

B.G. II, 19. (*a*) The first is to engage the rear of the enemy so as to delay their march, and give time for the main body to deploy and for the commander to form his plans. For this purpose a body of cavalry was sent forward, sometimes with the addition of light infantry.

B.G. I, 15,
21. (*b*) The second object is to reconnoitre the country (*loci naturam perspicere, iter cognoscere*), and to bring news of the enemy. To accomplish this, special detachments of the cavalry were sent forward (*exploratores*), who scoured the country far in front and on both flanks. To these A. 12. detachments were often assigned trusty staff-officers, accompanied by spies (*speculatores*).

B.G. II, 17. (*c*) The third object was to select and make ready the place for the camp. This duty was entrusted to a detail of centurions from the legions, accompanied by a few men, and usually under a tribune or some officer of the general staff.

§ **131.** At a fixed distance after the van marched the main body, and close after it the rear-guard. This last, during a march to the front, had only police duty to perform ; *i.e.*, to pick up stragglers, and the like.

§ **132.** The main body may march in one of three forms : *a.* In column, each legion accompanied by its baggage ;

b. In column, all the baggage of the army together; *c.* In line of battle. We will consider these in their order.

§ **133.** *a.* This form of march was only adopted in a B.G. II, 17 friendly country, or when there appeared no immediate danger of an encounter with the enemy. The legions are in single column, the cohorts in column of centuries with single or double number of ranks, according to the width of the road. Each legion is followed immediately by its baggage, which thus divides it from the legion next following. The last legion probably detached a few cohorts to follow the baggage. This detachment would thus form the rear guard of the whole army. A column of five legions in this order, with a breadth of 40 ft., requires 10,250 ft., or 4100 steps (*gradus*) in length. A sixth legion would need 40 minutes to reach the head of this column so as to join in battle. Of course if the march was with double number of ranks, so much more time would be taken.* It is clear that if the enemy could make a vigorous attack in force on the head of the column, they would have a good chance to throw it into confusion and entirely prevent it from properly deploying.

The legions marching in this order, each followed by its baggage, cannot be called ready for battle (*expeditae*).

§ **134.** *b.* When near the enemy, if it is not desirable to B.G. II 19 march in order of battle, the column is formed as in *a*, but 25, 26. the baggage of the whole army is assembled. The greater part of the legions, usually three-fourths of the entire number, composes the head of the column. Then followed the collected baggage. The remaining legions, usually one-fourth of all, brought up the rear (*claudunt agmen*), as guard for the baggage and rear-guard for the army. In this

---

* See *ante*, § 84.

B.G. II, 19; order the legions can much more rapidly be deployed, and
V, 2; VII, may properly be called *expeditae*.
40; C. I, 64.

Although the legions can readily be brought into action, we cannot consider them as actually ready until the individual soldiers have made their preparations. On the march, the soldier had to carry his personal baggage (*sarcinae*). Also, his heavy helmet was hanging at his breast, his shield was in a leather case, his field badges (*insignia*), plumes, and the like, carefully protected from the dust.

Then if a legion marching *expedita* is attacked in the march (*in agmine, sub sarcinis, in itinere*), before being able to meet the enemy the legionaries must first pile their
B.G. I, 24; baggage (*sarcinae in acervum comportantur, sarcinae con-*
VII, 18; A. *feruntur*), draw the shields from their coverings (*tegimenta*
69.
B.G. II, 21. *scutis detrahuntur*), put on their field badges (*insignia*
B.G. II, 21; *accommodantur*), put on helmets (*galeae induuntur, galean-*
A. 12.
B.G.VII, 18. *tur*), and get their weapons ready (*arma expediuntur, legio armatur*). Of course time was needed for all this, and time must be won by the vanguard. An enterprising enemy, knowing these facts, would seek to attack the Roman army
B.G. II, 17; on the march (*sub sarcinis adoriri, impeditos in agmine*
III, 24; C. *adoriri*), and meanwhile give as little time as possible for
I, 66; A. 75. making the proper preparations to resist.

§ 135. *c.* The advance in order of battle (*acie instructa*) could occur only for short distances. We find it made on two occasions for a distance of 16,000 steps, or about three hours' time. This formation could only be employed when in the immediate vicinity of the enemy, and when the ground was suitable.

When marching in order of battle, the legions marched in columns, as has been explained under the tactics of the legion. And when in this order it is clear that the men
B.G. VIII, must all be ready for immediate battle (*legiones armatae et*
36. *instructae*). This alone would prevent a march to any

great distance, as the baggage (*sarcinae*) must all be left in camp.

2. THE RETREAT.

§ **136.** A retreat in presence of the enemy is less convenient than an advance. It was usually in one of two forms : *a.* The retreat in column, with baggage massed ; *b.* The retreat in square (*agmine quadrato*).

§ **137.** *a.* For the retreat in column, the baggage was C. III, 75, sent out of camp as soon as possible, under escort of a de- 77. tachment of infantry, often of an entire legion. This body would constitute the vanguard. With them marched a detail of centurions and men whose business was to stake out the new camp.

Then followed the main body, the cohorts in column of centuries. Finally, at a suitable distance followed the rear guard (*agmen novissimum*).

It was the duty of these last to delay the enemy, thus giving the army time to push on, or to deploy, if the attack should be made in force. The rear-guard was composed of B.G. I, 24. cavalry, with archers and slingers. When necessary, they would be supported by troops from the legions. Sometimes the *antesignani*, and again legionary cohorts ready for battle C, III, 75; (*expeditae*), or even entire legions, marched between the A. 75. main body and the rear-guard. Often the legions did this duty by turns (*legiones invicem ad extremum agmen* A. 70. *evocabat*).

§ **138.** *b.* The retreat in square (*agmen quadratum*) was B.G.VII,67 chosen when surrounded by the enemy ; for instance, on a march through a rebellious country, and also when the enemy had numerous cavalry. A single square could be formed from all the legions, with the united baggage of the army in the centre ; or, each legion could form a square by itself, with its baggage within. This last would be the mode when the army was originally marching in column with divided baggage, and was compelled to make front suddenly on all sides, without time for the baggage to assemble. But *one* square of all the legions seems to have been customary. The cavalry, supported by the archers and slingers and by the *antesignani*, remained outside the square, and skirmished around it on all sides.

3. THE MARCH TO THE FLANK.

§ **139.** Flank marches were made only for a short distance, and always in order of battle. The legions marched in a column of lines, so that there would be two or three parallel columns, according to the formation.

C. III, 67;
B.G. I, 49.

§ **140.** The baggage train would either march on the side opposite the enemy, or between the legions, each being followed by its own pack-animals. The latter mode might be used when the army was divided from the enemy by some considerable obstacle, like a river, or when the side remote from the enemy was difficult to traverse; for instance, when the army was marching in the valley of a stream, so that the water was on the flank towards the enemy, and hills and woods on the other flank. In such case as last mentioned, no guard of light troops would be necessary between the army and the enemy. But in open ground such a detachment would have to be made, and would perform the same duties as the vanguard during an advance, and the rear-guard during a retreat.

A. 67.

B.G. VII,
34-36.

§ **141.** To form line of battle from a column of march by the flank was a simple matter, unless the baggage was between the legions. It was done simply by facing right or left, as the case might be.

§ **142.** In every march of a large body of troops the order of march was changed daily, and the legions daily

P. VI, 40.

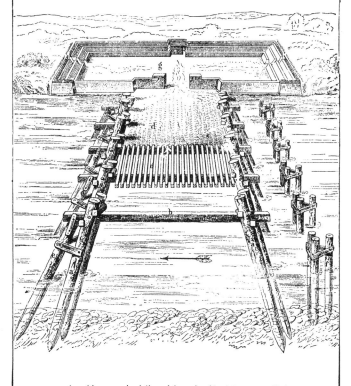

PONS A CÆSARE IN RHENO FACTUS

a a. tigna bina sesquipedalia.   b b. trabes bipedales.   c c. fibulae.
d d. directa materia, longuriis cralibusque constrata.
e e. sublicae ad inferiorem partem fluminis pro ariete oblique actae.
f f. sublicae supra pontem immissae.
g. castellum ad caput pontis positum.

Fig. 26.

took turns in leading, so that each in turn might come first
to the camp.

4. CROSSING STREAMS.

§ **143.** Rivers were crossed either by *fords* or by *bridges*.
The Romans could cross deeper fords than we, as they had
no powder to keep dry. Cæsar preferred fords whenever
practicable, as they required no previous preparation. Some-
B.G. VII, 56. times an artificial ford was made. Often, when the current
was strong, a line of cavalry was stationed up stream from
the point of crossing, and another line down stream, and the
infantry crossed in this shelter. The upper line of cavalry
broke the force of the current, and the lower line saved any
men who were carried from their footing.

§ **144.** When fords were not available, bridges had to be
built. These were of many kinds. The simplest were to
cross a mere ravine, and consisted of long tree trunks covered with branches and earth. The most elaborate of
which we know was the footway 40 ft. wide with which
Cæsar twice spanned the Rhine. A river in Spain he
H. 5.   bridged by sinking baskets filled with stones, as foundations
for his piers. Other streams were crossed by bridges of
boats. A bridge of any importance had to be protected by
strong fortifications at each end; and, when it was desired
to retain it, these were held by suitable garrisons (*praesidia*).
B.G. IV, 17; Cæsar's bridges on the Rhine (Fig. 26) were of this
VI, 9.   description. They were masterpieces of military engineering, and were held securely while the army moved into
Germany.

C. THE CAMP.

§ **145.** The Romans distinguished two kinds of camp:
the field, or summer camp (*castra aestiva*), made at the
close of each day's march, to be abandoned the next morn-

ing ; and the winter camp (*castra hiberna*), in which the army spent the time between two campaigns.

§ **146.** We have no exact account of the camp in the time of Cæsar. Our only complete information on this subject, in fact, is of the time of the second Punic war, given by Polybius, and in the time of Trajan, by Hyginus. Rüstow interprets by the following rule : Whatever is com- R. p. 75. mon to both may be set down at once as true of Cæsar. Where the authorities differ, Hyginus may be preferred, as the organization of the army in the time of Polybius differed more from that of Cæsar than did Trajan's. However, Cæsar customarily used fewer auxiliaries than did Trajan.

I. The Summer Camp.

1. *The Site.*

§ **147.** When possible, the camp was always placed on the slope of a gentle hill, so that its front had before it still a portion of the descent, and its rear lay on the summit. Thus the legions could pour from the gates and form against an approaching enemy in readiness to make their favorite onset down hill (*ex loco superiore*). If at the foot of the B.G. I, 24; declivity was some obstruction, as a stream or a morass, it II, 5, 8, 24; was all the better. At any rate, there should be before the III, 19. camp room for the accustomed order of battle. Of course water was necessary. Therefore the camp was usually placed on the sloping side of the valley of some stream. If the army had to cross a river, the camp could be made on either side. But the conditions were usually best met by placing it on the hither side. Much wood, too, was needed, for cooking, and for the various uses to which it was put in the fortifications. But yet the camp must not be so near a forest as to allow the enemy to collect in numbers under its shelter, and then make a sudden onset.

§ **148.** It is evident that all these conditions could not always be fulfilled, and often a camp must be pitched where necessity demanded (*in loco necessario*). But to place the camp on low ground instead of on a hill was considered barbarous (*more barbaro*).

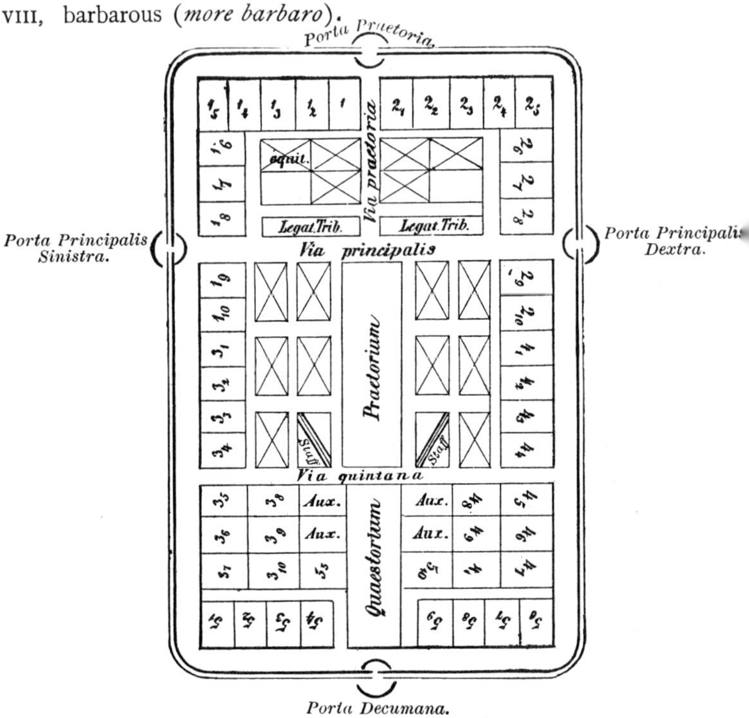

B.G. VIII, 36.

Porta Decumana.
Fig. 27. *The Summer Camp.*

NOTE. — 1_2 = First legion, second cohort, etc. This camp is planned for 5 legions, with cavalry and auxiliaries.

2. *The Fortification.* — *a.* THE GROUND PLAN.

R. pp. 75 seqq.

§ **149.** The right-angled quadrilateral was in Cæsar's time probably the only form of a Roman camp.* The quadrilat-

A. 80.

---

* The *castra lunata* mentioned at Thapsus was doubtless a series of rectangular camps, arranged in crescent form, with intervals, connected by wall and ditch.

eral was also the prevailing, if not the only, form of the small redoubts which among the Romans were known as *castella*, or *little camps*. We find these in the circumvallation of towns under siege, connected by lines of fortification. The *castella* very likely were quadrilaterals with side equal to the front of a cohort. They could then each be easily garrisoned and defended by one cohort.

The corners, both of *castra* and *castella*, were rounded, so as to afford more room for defence.

§ **150.** The gates of the camp were usually merely openings, probably as wide as the front of a maniple (40 ft.). They were defended by semi-circular *tambours*, or by a traverse (*titulum*) reaching to a corresponding distance. Very likely on the inside was a corresponding traverse. Usually the gates were not closed up. When it was neces- B.G. V, 5c sary to defend the camp, one or more of these might be closed, however. In small redoubts (*castella*), only a narrow opening was needed, and this might easily have had a real gate. In lines of fortifications, openings must be left at intervals for sorties.

b. THE ELEVATION.

§ **151.** The normal Roman fortification consists of a wall B.G. V, 39 (*agger, vallum*), on which the defenders place themselves; and before it a ditch (*fossa*), from which comes most of the material for the wall, and which keeps the enemy from approaching and stops them at the distance of a good spear cast (Fig. 28).

1. *The Ditch.*

§ **152.** Vegetius gives in two places the size of a ditch. V. I, 24. In the one which is more like those found in Cæsar, he III, 8. speaks of a ditch whose width at the top was 9 or 12 ft., and whose depth in the first case was 7 ft., and in the latter was 9 ft., vertically downward (*sub linea*).

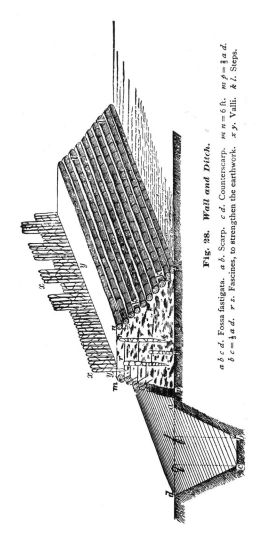

Fig. 28. *Wall and Ditch.*

a b c d. Fossa fastigata. *a b.* Scarp. *c d.* Counterscarp. *m n* = 6 ft. *m p* = ⅓ *a d.* *b c* = ⅓ *a d.* *r s.* Fascines, to strengthen the earthwork. *x y.* Valli. *k l.* Steps.

We notice that the width is in each case divisible by 3, and that the depth is two-thirds of the width, plus 1.

Cæsar often speaks of ditches whose width is divisible by 3, of 12, 15, and 18 ft., for instance; and only once, in the works at Alesia, of 20 ft. Further, Cæsar gives always only one dimension of the ditch. This would seem to imply that the other dimensions stood invariably in a fixed ratio to the one given.* He gives expressly both dimensions of his ditches only when they are unusual. For the customary fortification of a camp, it seems likely that the width was 9 ft., and the depth 7. Figure 28 is to be interpreted as follows : —

B.G. **VII**. 27, 72. C. I, 41.

 ab is the escarpment or scarp. *bc* is the bottom.
 cd is the counterscarp. *qc* or *fb* is the vertical depth.

§ **153.** Hyginus speaks of two forms : the *fossa fastigata* (Fig. 28), in which both scarp and counterscarp are sloping ;

Fig. 29.

Fig. 30.

and the *fossa punica* (Fig. 29), with sloping scarp and vertical counterscarp. Cæsar adds a third form (Fig. 30), with vertical sides (*directis lateribus*) ; *i.e.*, both the scarp (*latus interius*) and the counterscarp (*latus exterius*) were vertical. This ditch had of course the same width at bottom as at top.

B.G. **VII**. 72.

§ **154.** We may infer that the *fossa fastigata* was the usual form, merely because generally earth would be apt to

---

 * Göler thinks that he named but one dimension because the other was always the same ; and that that uniform depth was most likely 9 ft., because more than that would render it difficult to cast up the earth. But we must remember that the Romans relied much on baskets for carrying earth, rather than on the shovel alone.

cave in either of the others. Modern engineering makes the slope of the scarp greater than that of the counterscarp, the better to oppose the fire of artillery. But the fortifications of the ancients had little to fear from missiles ; so it seems probable that scarp and counterscarp had the same slope.

§ 155. Remembering that the width ad is always divisible by 3, it at once seems likely that one-third the width is to be reckoned for af, one-third for dq, and the remaining one-third for qf, or its equal, bc. Then the depth qc is equal to $2 \times cb + 1$. The area of the vertical section of such a ditch is $2 cb (2 cb + 1)$ sq. ft. Or, representing one-third of ad by x, $qc = (2x + 1)$ ft., and the area of the vertical section $abcd$ $= 2x (2x + 1)$ sq. ft. Thus for each running foot in the length of the ditch, there would be $2x (2x + 1)$ cu. ft. of earth for the construction of the wall.

R. p. 86.

2. *The Wall.*

§ 156. We think of a wall mainly as a breastwork, behind which soldiers are sheltered from the fire of the enemy. But it was quite different with the Romans. They had little need for shelter from missiles. What they aimed at mainly was a high position, inaccessible to the enemy, from which to hurl their spears.

§ 157. The section of such a wall we may consider practically a rectangle, *mnop* (Fig. 28), of sufficient height and width. The width *mn* should be enough to give room for standing firmly, and for moving backward and forward to hurl the javelins. Six feet would do. The height should be as great as possible, though of course this would be limited by the fact that the earth which formed the wall came from the ditch. Of course if towers were placed on the wall, the latter had to be made wider. The usual height seems to have been two-thirds of the upper width of the ditch. Cæsar often speaks of a ditch 15 ft. wide and a wall of 10 B.G. II, 5. ft., and the like.

§ **158.** The outer slope *mz* could be made very steep, as there was no fire of cannons to withstand. But to keep the earth of the wall in place, there must have been a facing of some more tenacious material. For this purpose there were used sods, cut in digging the ditch ; also timber and brush. This last was put up in bundles, in the form that we call fascines.

§ **159.** Vegetius says that the Romans cut sods $1\frac{1}{2}$ ft. V. III, 8. long, 1 ft. wide, $\frac{1}{2}$ ft. thick, for use in fortifications. Two such sods, packed one on the other, gave a height of 1 ft. to the facing for each foot in the length of the wall ; assuming the sods to have been placed endwise to the wall. Every 3 ft. in the width of the ditch gave two such sods, or a foot high of the facing. Then from a ditch 9 ft. wide could be cut 6 sods to the running foot, or 3 ft. in height of facing. With these sods one-half the height of the wall could be faced, leaving the other half to be strengthened with sod cut elsewhere, or with fascines.

§ **160.** The Romans were not always content with this facing of the outer slope. When they sought to give the wall especial height, they made it firmer by several lines of wicker work, or hurdles, *rs*, *tu*, parallel to the length.

§ **161.** Then the rampart must be easily mounted from the inside. For this purpose steps were made, *kl*. These were of brush, or at least strengthened with brush. So it was clear that a Roman camp needed much wood ; and also that the section of the wall was greater than the section of the ditch.

§ **162.** The vertical section of a wall 6 ft. in height and width, well faced, and provided with steps, contains about 56 sq. ft. The ditch (*fossa fastigata*), 9 ft. wide and 7 ft. deep, has a section of 42 sq. ft. But the earth would loosen itself about one-sixth in digging. That gives 49 sq. ft. section for the earthwork, leaving 7 sq. ft. for brushwork. Of this, at least 6 sq. ft. must be allotted to the steps

B.G. V, 40; VII, 72.

§ **163.** When the wall was wide enough, on its top was placed a breastwork (*lorica, loricula*) of stakes (*valli*), with only a few twigs left, which were firmly bound together. This breastwork was either of a uniform height of 4 to 5 ft., so that the soldiers could easily see over it and cast their spears, or there were pinnacles (*pinnae*) placed on it, 2 or 3 ft. high, between which were gaps.

§ **164.** There were often erected on the wall, from point to point, wooden towers. At such points both wall and B.G. V. 40; ditch had to be wider. Sometimes there were two ditches VII, 72. at such places.

§ **165.** Cæsar at his camp against the Bellovaci had two ditches with vertical sides, 15 ft. wide. If these were 11 ft. deep, they would yield 385 cu. ft. of earth for each foot in the length of the wall. A wall 12 ft. high could here have a width of 24 ft. including the outer slope and the steps. On such a wall could be placed towers with a square base of 16 to 20 ft. on a side, yet leaving a passage round them of 8 to 4 ft. wide. As such a tower must exert a considerable pressure on the side of the ditch, a space of at least a foot must have been left between the ditch and the foot of the wall.

3. *The Interior.*

§ **166.** The camp was generally a square, or a rectangle whose sides were as 2 to 3 (Fig. 27). The *front* was the side towards the enemy, or towards which on the following day the march would be taken up.* The *rear* was of course opposite, and the other two sides were right and left to one facing the front.

§ **167.** The depth of the camp was divided into three nearly equal parts. Beginning at the front, they were the *praetentura*, the *latera praetorii*, and the *retentura*. These three divisions were made by two broad streets, parallel to the front, the *via principalis* and the *via quintana*. The former ends at each side of the camp with a gate, the *porta principalis dextra* and the *porta principalis sinistra*. Very likely in large camps there were gates at the ends of the *via quintana* also. B.G. III, 19 V, 58; VII, 41.

§ **168.** In the middle of the front wall is the *porta prae-* *toria ;* and opposite, in the rear wall, is the *porta decumana*. B.G. II, 24; III, 25; C. III, 76.

§ **169.** From the *porta praetoria* to the *via principalis* extends a street, the *via praetoria*. Opposite this, in the middle part of the camp, is the *praetorium*, a wide space, in which were the headquarter tents, the altars, and the tribunal. This space occupies in length all the middle of the camp, but extends only 100 or 150 ft. each side of the middle line. C. III, 82.

§ **170.** In the *retentura* was a similar place, the *quaes-* *torium*. Here were the quarters of the administrative staff, here hostages and prisoners were kept, and forage and booty were placed. Outside of the camp, back of the *porta decu-* *mana*, were the booths of the sutlers (*mercatores*) who followed the army. B.G. VI, 37.

§ **171.** In the *praetentura* were stationed from one-fourth to one-fifth of cohorts, equally divided between the two sides. These cohorts occupied the tents facing the wall.

---

* But see Nissen, Das Templum, p. 23 seqq.

Also in the *praetentura*, along the *via principalis*, facing this and the middle of the camp, was the place for the tents of the *legati* and *tribuni militum*. Again, in each half of the *praetentura*, in the space enclosed by the cohorts along the wall, by the tents of the *legati* and *tribuni*, and by the *via principalis*, were encamped one-fourth of the cavalry and one-half of the archers and slingers. Thus in the entire *praetentura* were quartered one-half of the cavalry and all the archers and slingers, ready to move from the front gate and form the advanced guard.

§ **172.** On each flank of the *mid-camp*, next the wall, was a line of cohorts : on each side one-tenth of the entire number in the army, or one-fifth altogether. Next the *prætorium*, along both its longer sides, were placed the staff, except, of course, the *legati* and *tribuni*. Between the cohorts that were along the wall and the staff troops, were encamped on each side one-fourth of the cavalry, or one-half in the whole mid-camp. Their front was towards the *via principalis*, unless there were gates at the ends of the *via quintana*. In that case one-half (or one-fourth of the whole) would front toward each street, and they would be ready to rush out at either side.

B.G. V, 50, 58.

In the rear part of the camp, on each side of the *quaestorium* and equally divided by it, lay the rest of the cohorts, about one-half of all in the army. Their front was towards the wall on the flanks and rear. Enclosed by these, by the *quaestorium*, and by the *via quintana*, was the place for the auxiliary infantry, excepting the archers and slingers.

§ **173.** Entirely around the camp, within the wall, extended a broad street. This would at once prevent the likelihood of hostile missiles reaching the tents, and would allow room for moving troops to defend the walls. Polybius gives the width of this as 200 ft., and Hyginus, as 60. The latter seems too small for all the movements of an energetic defence. As we know that in Cæsar's time much stress was laid on skill in defending the camp, we may conclude that this street was quite wide, probably at least 120 ft.

4. *Arrangement of the Cohorts.*

§ **174.** The order in camp naturally depends on the order of march. It seems reasonable to conclude that this was usually in column of centuries. Hyginus gives the arrangement of a cohort of six centuries.

§ **175.** The cohort encamped in a space of 120 ft. front and 180 ft. depth. This was divided on lines parallel to the front into 6 portions of 120 ft. by 30 ft. Each of these was for one century.

From the length of the front, 12 ft. are to be deducted for the street dividing the cohort from the adjacent one. That leaves 108 ft. for the tents. Each century had 8 tents : 6 for the soldiers, 1 for the centurion, and 1 for the servants. As each tent is 10 ft. square, the length actually covered by tents would be 80 ft. This leaves 28 ft. for the 7 intervals between the tents, or 4 ft. for each interval. The 3 first centuries of the 3 maniples had their front towards the wall, and the 3 second their front from the wall. Thus the 2 centuries of one maniple would be stationed back to back. The second of one maniple would face the first of the next, divided from it by a street 12 ft. wide, parallel to the wall.

§ **176.** From the 30 ft. depth of the space allotted to the century, 6 ft. must be allowed for their half of the street ; 10 ft. for the tents ; 5 ft., behind the latter, for stacking the weapons ; and, finally, 9 ft. for the pack-animals. The C. III, 76. several cohorts of a legion, according to the room, could be placed in a line, side by side, or in several lines.

5. *Arrangement of the Cavalry in Camp.*

§ **177.** In camp there would suffice for each *turma* a space of 120 ft. by 30 ft., the same as for a century of infantry. Then one *ala* of cavalry would take the same room, and be arranged in the same way, as two cohorts of infantry. Of course in particulars the arrangement must have been varied to adapt it to the convenience of that arm of the service.

6. *Time needed for Fortifying the Camp.*

R. pp. 90, 91. § **178.** Let us assume the normal measure of the ditch to be 9 ft. wide and 7 ft. deep. Of course a part of the men must be under arms. We may suppose that, under all ordinary circumstances, in a body of troops of at least two legions, the men of one cohort could be used for each 240 ft. of wall. In digging a ditch of 9 ft. wide, in 240 ft. length not more than 60 men can conveniently work. Then in the same space allot 30 men to the wall, and 30 men to make the fascines and gather material, and we see that an equal number are at work on wall and ditch, and the two go on at an equal rate. As 120 men compose the normal strength of the maniple, and as there are three maniples, it is clear that there could be three reliefs. A relief of the ditch-diggers would be necessary, but it would hardly be so with the rest. Remembering that there were always some soldiers who were exempt from such work (*immunes, beneficiarii*), there might be in a maniple 100 men disposable for the work of fortifying. Then there could easily be three details for digging the ditch, with men to spare.

§ **179.** A skilful digger, who works only one hour and is then relieved, can easily excavate from 50 to 60 cu. ft. (Roman) in that time. But the Roman legionaries were above all things skilful at digging. As the cross-section of the ditch was $4\frac{1}{2}$ sq. ft., and each of the 60 men in one relief had a length of 4 ft. to excavate, there would be for each man in the relief, or at least for 3 men, one in each

Fig. 31. Fortifying the Camp.

MOSS ENG. CO. N.Y.

relief, 168 cu. ft. to throw out. This was the work of from 3 to 4 hours. Then, if the camp was begun at noon, by 4, or, at the latest, 5 P.M., the fortification would be complete.

7. *Camp Duties.*

§ **180.** When the van of the army reacned the camp-ing-ground selected, it was immediately formed with front towards the enemy to cover the work of fortification. Strong details of cavalry reconnoitred in all directions, while the engineers set to work immediately at measuring C. III, 13. and staking out the camp. As the legions arrived, they proceeded each to its allotted place, and laid aside baggage and arms (excepting swords) in the space behind the site C. III, 76. for the tents (*arma in contubernio deposita*). The cohorts assigned to guard duty of course retained their arms, and proceeded at once to their posts. Baggage and arms being laid aside, the legions marched to the wall street, and were there told off, some for work within the camp, some for fortifying. The latter work, having been already measured B.G. II, 19. (*opere dimenso*), was begun at once (*castra ponuntur,* B.G. I, 49; *muniuntur*). When the baggage train arrived, the ani-II, 5, 13. C. mals were unloaded by the servants (*calones*). The tents I, 81. as a rule were only pitched when the fortifications were completed. When not near the enemy, however, and especially in stormy weather, the tents would be pitched C. I, 80, 81. (*tabernacula constituere, statuere*) immediately on arrival.

§ **181.** As soon as the fortifications were finished, the bulk of the cavalry was withdrawn into the camp. A few B.G. V, 50. squadrons were left on picket without (*equites in statione*), B.G. II, 11; and these sent scouts (*exploratores*) in all directions. Any III, 2; VII, 44. special duty of gaining information was performed by spies B.G. II, 11; (*speculatores*). V, 49.

§ **182.** One cohort of each legion was usually placed on guard at each gate (*cohors in statione ad portam*). In B.G. IV, 11; the daytime, few sentries were posted. But during the night VI, 37; C. doubtless each cohort on guard lined the redan before the I, 75. gate, and its side of the wall, thickly with sentinels. Of course in special cases the guard was strengthened. Besides the guards at the gates, one cohort at least was detailed for duty in the camp, and was stationed in the *praetorium* and *quaestorium*.

§ 183. As soon as the fortification was completed, the supper was prepared and eaten. For this purpose the staff assembled in the *praetorium*, and remained until nightfall. Livy, The general during this time could conveniently promulgate XXXVI, 5 orders for the night and for the next day. At nightfall, also, the musicians of the army assembled to sound the tattoo. Livy,

This was the signal for setting the night watch. The XXX, 5. cavalry pickets were drawn into camp, except a few single horsemen as outlying sentries (*speculatores*). The guard B.G. II, 11 cohorts were probably changed at the tattoo, the new guard going on duty now to serve 24 hours. The night sentries (*vigiles*) were at once posted on the tambours (*titula*) and B.G. VIII, wall. The night, from sunset to sunrise, was divided into 4 35. equal watches (*vigiliae*). Each cohort on guard was divided accordingly into 4 reliefs, one of which should be on duty during each watch. The other 3 reliefs could rest, of course, on their arms. If the cohort contained only about 300 men, it will readily be seen that 70 men could compose one relief. This number, for 2100 ft. of wall, would give one sentinel for each 30 ft. The different reliefs were signalled by the trumpeters (*buccinatores*). C. II, 35.

§ 184. At daybreak the musicians sounded the reveillé. If the march was not to be resumed, the guard cohorts drew in their night sentries and posted the less numerous sentinels for the day. The cavalry pickets took their posts (*stationes*), and sent out their scouts (*exploratores*). At noon this cavalry guard was relieved. Livy, XL, 33; V. III, 8

§ 185. During the night the rounds of the sentries were probably made by the centurions of the guard. On occasion, also, the tribunes on duty, and the general himself, would inspect the guard.

§ **186**. If camp should be made in the presence of a threatening enemy, the usual vanguard would not be enough to cover the operation. One or two legions would then be deployed in line of battle to keep off the enemy, and a third would do the work of fortifying.

B.G. I, 49;
C. I, 41.

§ **187**. The army might leave the camp either to attack a near enemy, or in order to continue the march.

a. In the first case, the tents were left standing, the baggage remained in its place, and a guard was left in charge. This guard might consist of a detail from each legion, or of entire legions. The latter would be likely to occur when there were legions of raw recruits present. These would naturally be left within the walls.

B.G. III, 26;
II, 8; C. I,
41, 64.

b. In case of continuing the march, the camp was abandoned. At the first signal (*signum profectionis*), the tents were struck ; at the second, they and the rest of the baggage were packed on the beasts (*vasa conclamantur*) ; at the third, the march began. To conceal the departure from the enemy, the signal might be omitted. Yet it was deemed a point of military honor to sound it.

C. III, 85.
C.III, 37, 75.

II. THE WINTER CAMP.

§ **188**. In winter quarters the Romans did not billet their soldiers in towns, but kept them together in winter camps (*castra hiberna*). When a portion of a town was needed, for strategical or other reasons, then the inhabitants had to leave, as we see in the case of Galba at Octodurus.

B.G. III, 1.

§ **189**. The general arrangement of the winter camp must have resembled that of the *castra aestiva*. There must have been the same fortifications and streets. But doubtless the convenience of the men was more regarded than when in the field. In place of tents (*tabernacula, pelles*), the winter camp afforded huts which gave better protection against wind and weather. The arms were doubtless kept in the huts, and the pack-animals in sheds. Also more room could be taken than in the field.

D. THE SIEGE.

§ **190.** The Romans were accustomed to assail strong-holds in three ways, — by blockade (*obsidio*), by assault (*oppugnatio repentina*), and by formal siege (*oppugnatio*). R. p. 137 seqq.

1. *Blockade* was used against places of great strength, especially if poorly provided with provisions ; and further if the location allowed a complete environment. B.G. VII, 36, 69.

2. *Assault* (*oppugnatio repentina*, Fig. 32) was made on places of smaller importance, with weak fortifications, and well supplied with food. Of course emergencies might lead to the same method of attack on very strong places. C. III, 80

3. *Formal siege* was resorted to against positions that were strongly fortified and well provisioned, so that neither of the preceding methods was of avail. B.G. VII 11.

I. BLOCKADE.

§ **191.** The blockade was accomplished by means of the circumvallation (*circumvallatio*). The besieged place was surrounded by fortifications. These consisted of strong redoubts (*castella*) at convenient places, connected by lines of wall and ditch (*munitiones, brachia*).* Outside of these lines lay the camp, or camps, of the blockading army. If an attempt at relief from without was to be feared, another line of works must be created, outside the first, and facing outwards. In modern warfare this latter line is called the *circumvallation*, and the inner one the *contravallation*. Cæsar does not use the latter term, and applies the former as has been explained. B.G. VII, 15.
C. III, 43; B.G. VII, 69.
B.G. VII, 68; C. III, 41.

---

* See Fig. 42.

Fig. 32. *Oppugnatio.*

a. Testudo aggestitia.   *b.* Testudo arietaria.   *c.* Turris ambulatoria.   *d.* Corvi.   *e.* Harpago.   *f.* Falx muralis.

NOTE.— This cut represents an attack both by land and water, in which no *agger* is employed. While in these respects unlike the attack on the Gallic towns, it shows very clearly some siege implements in actual use.

§ 192. It is clear that the strength that must be given to the fortifications depends upon the relative strength of besiegers and besieged. If the besiegers are weak, their works must be correspondingly stronger.

§ 193. The redoubts (*castella*) were held by garrisons (*praesidia*). These in the daytime merely threw out a line of sentries (*stationes*), which they were ready to support immediately. At night strong pickets (*excubitores*) occupied the works. In the redoubts were always ready the means of making signal—smoke by day, and fire by night—in case of attack. Constant watch was kept lest at any point a sortie might be made by the enemy. B.G. VII, 69; C, III, 65.

C. III, 65.

2. ASSAULT.

§ 194. The principal article used in assaults was the scaling-ladder. Breaching-huts (*musculi*, § 210) were also used. These were low, small houses with sloping roofs, and built of strong materials, to resist the showers of missiles from the wall. These were pushed forward on rollers, and under their shelter battering-rams (§ 213) were brought to bear on the wall. C. III, &c.

§ 195. As soon as the ladders were ready, the breaching-huts (§ 210), were built fascines and fagots were prepared for filling the ditch, and hurdles were made ready for protecting the archers and slingers.* These troops were then pushed forward, thus protected, in order to clear the walls of the defenders. Behind the missile troops were formed the legionaries, usually in several columns. Thus the attention of the enemy would be distracted, and at *one* of the points of attack success might follow. At the head of each column was a body of laborers with ladders and fascines. As soon as the archers and slingers had cleared the wall, the facines were cast into the ditch, the ladders were set up, and the

---

* Also see § 28.

legionaries mounted to the attack. If a lodgment was effected, the assailants sought to spread out each way and gain a gate, in order to open it to their comrades. Meantime the battering-ram was at work at various points, that no resource might be wanting.

3. Regular Siege.

R. p. 142 seqq.; B.G. II, 30; VII, 24; C. II, 1, 15.

§ **196.** The principal work of a regular siege was the mound (*agger*, Figs. 33, 34, 35). This was always begun at a distance from the wall, very nearly out of reach of missiles. It was then gradually extended in the direction of the point to be attacked, and was at the same time gradually increased in height until on a level with the top of the walls, or even higher. When this mound was completed, the storming party moved on its top to the attack.

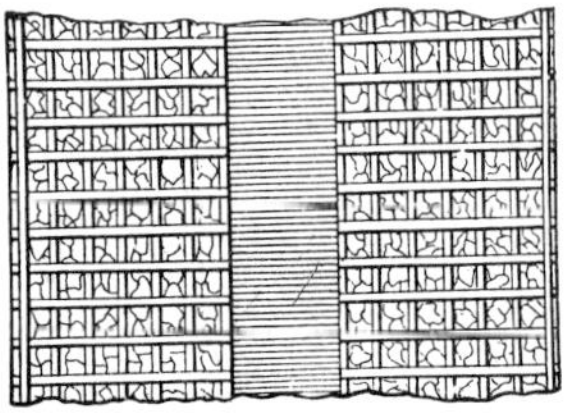

Fig. 33.
Horizontal Section of Agger.

§ **197.** The height of the mound was often considerable. Before Avaricum it was 80 ft., and as much before Massilia. The length of course depended on the power of the enemy's missile weapons. It seems probable that those built in assaulting the Gallic towns would not have been very long. The least distance from the enemy at which the construction could have been begun was from 400 to 500 ft.

§ **198.** The width above must have been enough for a storming column, very likely of the usual formation. If we take this to be the front of a maniple, the least breadth would have been 50 ft. The sides might be quite steep, as we shall see further on. A fabric 80 ft. high and 50 ft. wide on top might have been 60 ft. wide on the ground.

§ **199**. To the building of the *agger*, it must be remembered, everything else in the siege was subordinated.

By way of preparation for its construction, first of all the ground must be levelled for the foundation. This could be done by workmen protected by *vineae* (§ 211), stout movable sheds. Then the workmen, both those building the *agger* and those providing the material, must be guarded from the R.K. p. 310 missiles of the enemy. The former were protected by *plutei* (§ 214), large standing shields, which could be advanced C. II, 2. from time to time. The others brought the material in covered galleries. These were composed of a series of *vineae* B.G. II. 30; reaching to the point of beginning the *agger*. Also, the III, 21; C. II, 2. workmen were protected by archers, slingers, and artillery, drawn up parallel to the hostile walls. The archers and slingers were themselves protected by *plutei ;* the artillery B.G. II, 30; was placed usually in moving towers. These parallels must III, 21; VII, 17, 18; C. II, have had covered approaches of long lines of huts. Under 14. shelter of these, also, were posted bodies of legionaries (*cohortes expeditae*), to cover the operations and resist B.G. VII, sorties. Farther in the rear bivouacked strong bodies of 27. troops, outside the camp, ready to support. B.G. VII, 24.

§ **200**. The strength of the various protections would of course depend on the power of the enemy's missiles. Usually the side walls of the *vineae* were only of a sort of wattled work. Before Massilia, however, all the covering devices had to be made of logs of considerable thickness. C. II, 10.

§ **201**. Sometimes towers (*turres ambulatoriae*) were placed *on* the *agger*. In such cases the top of the *agger* was designed to be a smooth roadway ; and the height B.G. II, 30, needed only to be enough for the tower to have sufficient 31; VIII, 41. elevation. This probably was a quicker way of approach, as it saved building a considerable part of the *agger ;* but it was not so convenient for a column of attack. As a rule,

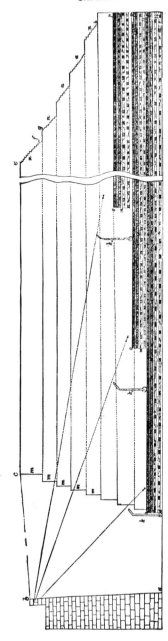

Fig. 34. *Vertical Section of Agger and Hostile Wall.*

a b c e f h n a. Entire section to be filled up. *c e f h n d.* Portion regularly constructed. *a b c d.* Portion filled at the last, helter skelter.
m n, m n, &c. Galleries through the different stories. *k k k.* Lines of *plutei.* *n n n*, &c. Steps. *f g*, &c. Platforms.

The lines of direction from the top of the wall show the spaces protected by the *plutei.*

however, the tower accompanied the construction of the *agger*, at its side ; and served as a battery to clear the enemy from the wall, and as a redoubt in the line of approaches

a. *Construction of the Agger.*

§ **202.** While we have no detailed accounts of the mode of building the *agger*, we do know the following facts : — R. p. 147 seqq.

1. That it contained much woodwork ; (*a*) because the *agger* was frequently set on fire by the enemy, and (*b*) because Trebonius was compelled to build a stone *agger*, for the reason, as he expressly states, that there was no more wood in the region. B.G. VII, 22, 24. C. II, 14. C. II, 15.

2. That this woodwork was not merely wattled branches, but was mainly logs (*arbores*, *materia*). C. II, 1, 15.

3. That it was not solid, but had holes, larger and smaller, which would admit a draft. This is inferred because it was sometimes set on fire from below, the enemy having driven a mine beneath it. G. VII, 24.

4. That it approached the wall gradually, and that the workmen, meanwhile, were protected from missiles. Thus it must have been erected one story at a time. B.G. VII, 24.

From these facts and necessary inferences, we may draw up a scheme of construction which cannot be far from the truth. C. II, 2, 15.

§ **203.** Figure 34 is a vertical, longitudinal section of the *agger*. *ab* is the city wall against which it is directed. The entire section of the *agger* when completed is *abcefhnda*. It is clear that only a portion of this, as *cefhnd*, can be constructed with regularity. The remainder, *abcd*, is so near the enemy that it must be filled up with a rush at the last moment. We speak first of the part that is constructed regularly.

§ **204.** The point of beginning must be as near the enemy as his missiles allow, — at some point in their long range.

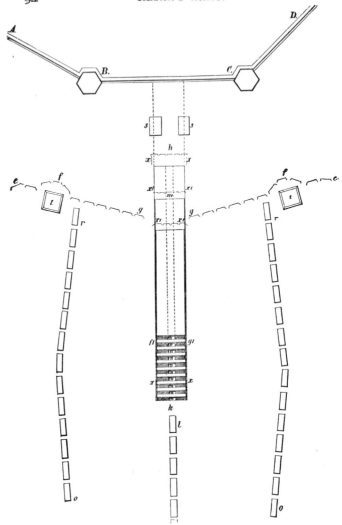

Fig. 35. General View of Siege Operations.

A B C D. Hostile wall. *s s. Testudines aggestitiae,* protecting those levelling the ground. *h k. Agger. x x, x x*, &c. *Plutei,* protecting those working on the *agger; e f g.* Line of *plutei,* manned with archers and slingers. *t t. Turres,* also manned with archers and slingers and provided with *tormenta. r o.* Covered way of *vineae,* giving approach to archers and slingers. *l q.* Covered way of *vineae* approaching the point of beginning the *agger. f g*. Position of *plutei,* covering the beginning of *agger. m n.* Covered gallery through the *agger. n n n,* &c. Steps and platforms of the several stories.

First of all a line of breaching-huts is moved forward so as to make a safe gallery through which to convey material. Then at a distance of perhaps 30 ft. in advance of this point is placed a line of large shields (*plutei, x*) at right angles to the line of huts, and longer than the width of the *agger*. These shields must be strong enough to turn the hostile missiles and high enough to protect the space of about 30 ft. between them and the huts. In this space thus protected the workmen set about the *agger*. The material with which they work consists principally of logs 20 to 30 ft. long, and from a foot to a foot and a half thick. These are piled, cob-house fashion, in successive courses, each course crossing the one below it at right angles. In the middle is left a passage (*mn*) 10 or 12 ft. wide. This passage when covered is to form a gallery through which is carried the material for continuing the work. The spaces between the logs are filled with stones, sods, and earth. When the structure has reached a height of about 7 ft., a course of logs (*op*) is placed close together across the whole. This at the same time covers the gallery and serves as a floor for the second story.

This completes 30 ft. of the first story. The shields (*plutei*) are now pushed on 30 ft. farther, and the work continued, material being brought through the line of huts and through the covered gallery in the portion of the *agger* already constructed. In like manner the work is pushed on by successive stages of 30 ft. each.

§ 205. Meanwhile at the point of beginning steps are made so as to mount easily to the second story. When the first story has advanced perhaps 100 ft., a transverse row of *plutei* (*k*) is placed on its flat roof, and a second story is begun and pushed on in like manner as the first. The beginning of the second story is far enough forward of the beginning of the first to leave a sufficient space, not merely for the steps, but also for a platform (*fg*) leading to the entrance (*n*) of the second gallery. Meanwhile, the outer sides are covered with green hides, as a protection against fire.

§ 206. Thus the work goes on, story by story, until the *agger* has reached the required height. Each story has its gallery running throughout its length, its platform, or landing, and steps leading to the story above.

§ 207. We come now to that part near the enemy's wall, which can only be made by pouring in material helter skelter. When the *agger* has reached a height of three or four stories, and has been brought as near the enemy as is consistent with the safety of the workmen, then a great quantity of rubbish, wood, bundles of straw, stones, sod, and the like, are brought through the various galleries and cast out through the openings (*m*), until the space between the *agger* and the wall is quite filled up.

§ 208. The great size of the *agger* is enough to show that wood was largely used in its construction. Then, too, wood is on the average only one-third as heavy as earth. It can therefore be gathered and transported more easily. Also, the side walls of a wooden *agger* can be much steeper than if of earth. An *agger* of earth, 50 ft. wide on the top and 80 ft. high, should be 210 ft. wide at the base, and therefore 130 ft. wide at the middle point of the height. One of wood would need to have an average width of only 55 ft.

An *agger* of earth of the above dimensions and 600 ft. long, would require 6,240,000 cu. ft. of earth. The mere *excavation* of this mass would take 1000 workmen at least 20 days.

b. Siege Apparatus.

§ 209. The principal work of a regular siege was the *agger*, by which safe approach was made to the hostile wall.

Subsidiary to this were various other means of protection and offence.

§ 210. The *musculus* was a hut, which could be moved on rollers, for the protection of workmen from the missiles of the besieged. There were two forms.

Fig. 36.

a. The first form (Fig. 36) was used by workmen engaged in levelling the ground for the *agger*, or in filling up the enemy's ditch. It was wedge-shaped, and built of strong

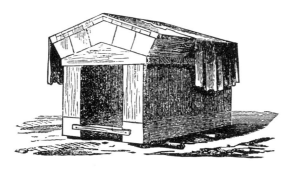

Fig. 37.

timbers covered by heavy planking. The forward end was constructed of two triangles put together, so that missiles would glance off.

b. The second form (Fig. 37) was used by pioneers who attempted to dig out the foundation stones of the hostile wall. As it came so near the enemy, it had to be very strong, to resist the heavy stones thrown down from the bat-

Fig. 38.

tlements. Those used in the siege of Massilia were probably 20 ft. long, 5 ft. high, and 4 ft. broad, built of timbers 2 ft. thick. Besides, the roof was covered with bricks and clay, to guard against fire, with hides over all, to prevent the clay being washed off by water.

C. III, 10.

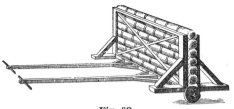

Fig. 39.

§ **211.** The *vineae* (Fig. 38) were huts, open at each end, designed to form a safe passage-way to the *musculus*, or to any point where the siege work was going on. As they were not brought so near the enemy as was the *musculus*, the *vineae* did not need to be so strong. By the description of Vegetius, the *vinea* was 16 ft. long, 8 ft. high, and 7 ft. wide, the side walls of strong posts connected by vaulted work, and the roof by a double thickness of planking. It will be seen that the *vinea* was more roomy than the *musculus*, being used merely

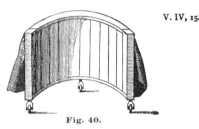

V. IV, 15.

Fig. 40.

as a passage-way. Often the roof was covered with green hides, to guard against fire

§ **212.** The *testudo* (Fig. 32, *b*) was a hut, much like the *musculus*, from the front of which, however, projected the battering-ram (*aries*). The ram was suspended from the roof of the hut, and was worked by a number of men thus protected.

§ **213.** The battering-ram*(*aries*, Fig. 32, *b*) was a long, heavy log of wood, the offensive end of which was strengthened by a head of metal (iron or bronze), sometimes in the shape of a ram's head. Suspended at its middle point from the roof of the hut (*testudo*), it was driven with considerable force against the wall. The ram has been found quite effective in disjointing stones, although its

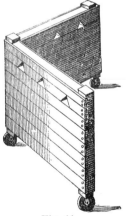

Fig. 41.

force is small compared with that of a cannon shot. The momentum of a ram 28 in. in diameter and 180 ft. long,

---

* See § 222, at end.

Fig. 42. *Section of Cæsar's Circumvallation at Alesia.*

ab = Pinnae.   *bc* = Lorica of Plutei.

NOTE.— The *Cippi* were branches of trees partly buried in trenches; the *lilia* (Fig. 43) were little pits with a sharp stake set in each, covered loosely with twigs and brush; the *stimuli* were sharp hooks projecting from the ground; the *cervi* were branches projecting horizontally from the wall.

weighing 41,112 lbs. and worked by 1000 men, is only equal to a point-blank shot from a 36-pounder.

§ 214. The movable tower (*turris ambulatoria*, Fig. 32, *c*) Cæsar used continually in his sieges. It rested on rollers, was several stories high, of truncated pyramidal shape, and constructed of heavy timbers. The stories were connected by stairs at the side remote from the enemy, and each floor was protected by a high bulwark. There were openings through which the archers and slingers could send their missiles. The tower was constructed out of range of the enemy, and then advanced on rollers, preceded by *musculi* containing workmen who leveled the road. The use of the tower was as a battery from which the opposing wall could be swept, thus protecting the workmen continuing the agger. Also when near enough, a bridge was let fall upon the wall from one of the upper stories, and thus soldiers could rush to the assault.

§ **215.** The *pluteus* (Figs. 39, 40, 41) was a movable shield, running on three wheels, one at each end and one in the middle. It was usually made of osier work covered with hides.

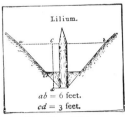

Fig. 43. *Lilium.*

VI. THE SHIPS AND SEA–FIGHTS.

3.G. III,
13–15; IV,
12–26,28,29;
V, 10, 11.
C. II, 3–7.
§ **216.** This subject belongs properly to a discussion of the Roman army, as the actual fighting on shipboard was always done by details from the legions.

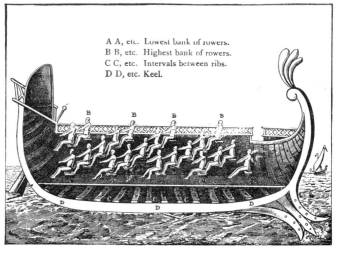

A A, etc. Lowest bank of rowers.
B B, etc. Highest bank of rowers.
C C, etc. Intervals between ribs.
D D, etc. Keel.

Fig. 44.*

Section of Galley with five Banks of Oars, showing the position of the rowers.

§ **217.** The Roman ships were propelled both by sails and oars. For the war-ships, however, the latter were the main reliance. The rowers (slaves) in a ship of any size sat under the deck, on benches arranged in tiers (Fig. 44). Each

---

* From Scheffer, *De Militia Navali Veterum*, Upsala, 1654 A.D.

rower was chained to his bench during his period of duty. The *working crew* of a war-ship comprised a few sailors to manage the sails and enough slaves to work the oars in reliefs, each usually working four hours at a time.* The galleys (*naves longae*) were very long and swift, having usually three tiers of oars. The *fighting crew*, as above said, consisted of a number of legionaries.

§ **218.** The war-ship was fitted with a beak (*rostrum*) of bronze at the prow. With this it was attempted to run down and sink a hostile ship. There was usually a detachment of slingers and archers on board, and a supply of artillery. Towers were sometimes raised on the deck, so as to send missiles down among the enemy. This was especially the case when a low ship was attacking a higher one. When two ships grappled, the legionaries boarded with shield and sword.

The galleys were of so light draft that they could be drawn up on the beach. Of course the largest ships of the Romans would be very small to modern eyes.

§ **219.** The distinction between military and naval science is of quite recent origin. Even so late as the seventeenth century A.D. the same men were employed on land or sea as might be most convenient. That staunch old Puritan admiral, Blake, who made the arms of the commonwealth as much feared on the sea as Cromwell did on land, was originally an officer of cavalry, — thus being a veritable "horse marine."

---

* For a vivid modern description of slave life in an ancient galley, see Wallace's *Ben Hur*, Bk. III.

VII. THE ENEMY.

A. DEFENCE OF FORTIFIED TOWNS.

§ **220.** The sieges that Cæsar's armies conducted were
against two sorts of fortifications, — the walled towns of the
Gauls, as Alesia, and the more elaborate works that defended haunts of Graeco-Roman civilization, like Massilia.

B.G. II, 12. § **221.** The former were comparatively simple, and fell
usually without much difficulty before the resources of
C. II, 1–15. Roman military science. The defences of Massilia, however, had been planned by the same engineering skill that
assailed them, and the town was supplied with every appli-
ance of resistance known to the military art of the day.
The siege of that city was a grapple of giants.

B.G.VII,23. § **222.** Cæsar gives a clear account of the construction
of a Gallic town wall.   Logs are laid on the ground, two

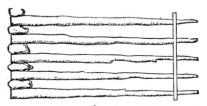

Fig. 45. *Horizontal Section of Gallic Wall.*

feet apart, their length at right angles to the direction of the
wall (Fig. 42).   The large end of each log is turned without, the small end within.   These smaller ends are then
fastened together by cross-timbers some 40 feet long, and
earth is piled on them.   Between the large ends are placed

great stones, and a rubble of small stones is poured into the
remaining space between the large stones and the earth at
the smaller ends of the logs. Then a second course of logs
is laid in like manner, only so that each log of this second
course was placed over the stones filling the space between
two logs of the first course. Thus the work is carried on
until the wall has reached the desired height. Such a wall
was quite effective. The stones protected it from fire, and
the timber, firmly bound together as it was, made it quite
secure from the battering-ram.

Perhaps this is why Cæsar so seldom mentions the ram in detailing R. p. 146.
his sieges. Rüstow says that Cæsar nowhere speaks of that implement.
This statement is an error, as reference is made in two places. B.G. II, 32;
VII, 23.

On the walls, towers were often erected at various points.

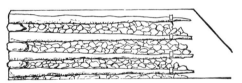

Fig. 46. *Vertical Section of Gallic Wall.*

§ 223. In the siege of Massilia we learn the varied resources of defence, only a few of which were known to the
Gauls.

In the first place, the rampart was lined with artillery, so
that the besiegers had to push on their works under a B.G. VII,
shower of stones and darts. Every effort was made to set 22–28.
C. II, 7-15.
fire to the *agger* and to the various huts. At Massilia this
at one time succeeded, and all the offensive works were consumed. Fire-balls, made of tow soaked in pitch and kin-
dled, were hurled from the wall. Mines were run, beginning
within the wall and ending in the siege works. Through
these mines the besieged made sudden sorties, trying to get
possession of the works and set them on fire. If the ram

was brought to bear on the wall, fenders were let down from its top by ropes to protect the stonework ; and it was sought by great hooks to catch the ram and draw it from its fastenings. As the *agger* and towers increased in height, the town wall and towers were often carried up to correspond. If the wall was itself successfully assailed and began to crumble, another wall was rapidly constructed on the inside. If all these things failed, however, and at last a clear way was made for assault, the town usually surrendered.

B. THE GALLIC ARRAY AND ARMS.

§ 224. The Macedonian phalanx had a front of about 500 men and a depth of 16. That of the Gauls and Germans was doubtless of similar form, but of varying numbers. The men stood close together, forming a compact mass. The shields of the front rank formed a vertical wall, and those of the rest were held overhead, lapping over one another like the shingles on a roof, only in the reverse order. It will be seen that the phalanx depended for its success on the momentum of its mass. However, only those on its outer edges could use their weapons, while the rest were practically imprisoned in the crowd. Here the Romans had a great advantage ; for, from their open and pliable order of battle, nearly every man sooner or later was in action. Hence, although they might be greatly inferior in number, they could bring into use more swords and spears at a given point than could their enemies.

At the battle of the Alma (fought Sept. 20, 1854), the British troops in line were attacked by heavy bodies of Russians in solid squares, not unlike the old phalanx. It seemed that if the huge mass of Russians should ever reach the thin British line (only two or three men deep), the latter would be shivered like a pipe-stem. But the impact never took place. Every one of the British was free to use his rifle, while in the square only the few men on the outer edges could do any firing. The result was that the squares were broken, their momentum destroyed, they gradually ceased their advance and finally retreated. (Kinglake's Invasion of the Crimea, Vol. III, p. 114 seqq.)

Such a defence in line against an opposing mass can only be made successfully by troops of considerable individual self-reliance. Such was the case undoubtedly with the British regiments at the Alma. Such was the case with Cæsar's legionaries. And so the open order of battle of the Romans, bringing every soldier to bear on the enemy, was possible, and was much more economical of force than the crowded phalanx of the Gauls.

It should be noticed, in this connection, that modern improvements in missile weapons are causing radical changes in tactics. Breechloading and repeating rifles have put an end to all solid formations in actual battle. In 1871, at St. Privat, the German army in 30 minutes lost one-third of its strength under the fire of the Chassepot rifles, although at distances from the French infantry ranging from half a mile to a mile and a quarter. In 1878 a Russian brigade attempted a bayonet charge on a Turkish redoubt in the Skuptschina Pass. The redoubt was manned by infantry armed with the American Remington rifle — and the brigade was annihilated in 15 minutes.

Since these wars, it is evident that the old tactics must be revolutionized. The skirmish line becomes the main reliance. More and more will depend on the intelligence of the individual. Of late, too, successful experiments have been made in the use of dynamite shells. This destroys the last possibility of mass formations.

Thus the experience of the Romans is repeated in our own day. Modern discoveries and inventions applied to military science demand a more open order of battle, and tend steadily to replace the brute force of a mob by scientific skill.

It is plain enough from this that Upton's Tactics is already obsolete. A Board is now sitting to devise a new system for the army of the United States.

§ 225. The Gallic sword was very long, two-edged, and sheathed in an iron scabbard that was suspended at the right side by an iron or bronze chain. This sword had no point, and hence was adapted rather for cutting than thrusting. The spear had a blade at least 2 ft. long and 6 to 8 in. wide, sometimes of an undulated form. As missile weapons, light javelins, bows, and slings were used. The helmet was of metal, adorned with the horns of animals, having a crest representing a bird or savage beast, and surmounted by a high and bushy plume of feathers. The shield was of plank, at least 5 ft. long, and very narrow. The body was guarded besides by an iron or bronze breastplate, or by a coat of mail. This last was a Gallic invention.

C. THE BRITISH CHARIOTS.

B.G. IV, 33. **§ 226.** In Britain, Cæsar met a new kind of attack. The squadrons of hostile cavalry were intermingled with chariots (*essedae*), two-wheeled cars, each drawn by two horses and containing six soldiers (*essedarii*) besides the driver (*auriga*). Their custom was to charge fiercely, hoping by the rush of their horses and the clatter of their wheels, as well as by the spears hurled by the *essedarii*, to throw their enemy into confusion. Failing this, they returned to a position among the squadrons of cavalry; and there the spearmen dismounted and took their post as footmen. Meanwhile the drivers took the chariots to the rear, and there waited.

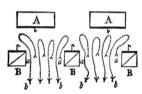

Fig. 47.

A A. Roman Legions.
B B B. British Cavalry.
a a a. Post of *essedarii.*
b b b. Post of chariots.
ab, etc. Course of chariots.

MAPS

OF THE PRINCIPAL CAMPAIGNS

AND

PLANS

OF THE MOST IMPORTANT BATTLES AND SIEGES
OF THE GALLIC WAR.

ADAPTED FROM

NAPOLEON'S LIFE OF CÆSAR.

GALLIA
ANTIQUA

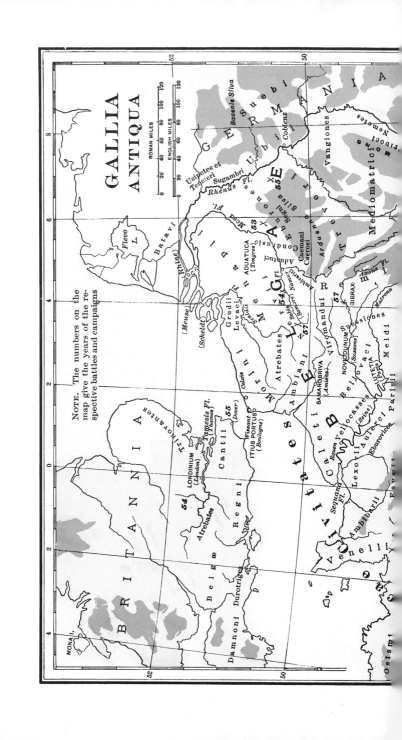

GALLIA
ANTIQUA

ROMAN MILES

ENGLISH MILES

NOTE. The numbers on the
map give the years of the re-
spective battles and campaigns

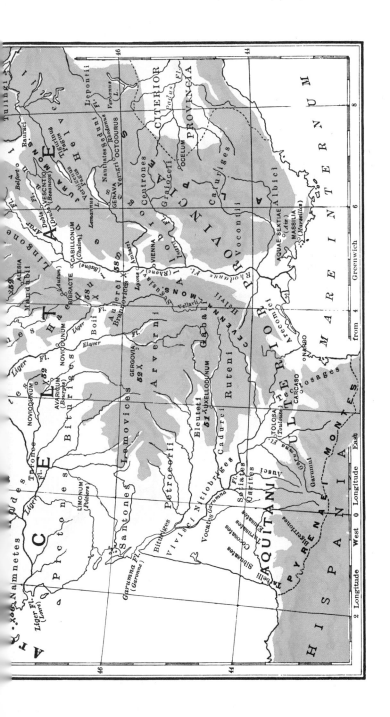

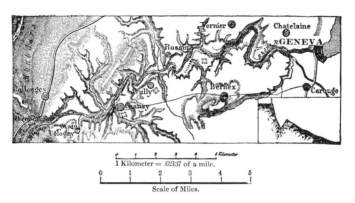

1 Kilometer = .62137 of a mile.

Scale of Miles.

Plan I. *Fortifications on the Rhone.* B.G., Bk. I. Chap. 8.

The dotted *lines* indicate wall and trench; the dotted *squares*, redoubts. In the lower corner at the right is a vertical section of *murus* and *fossa*. From Geneva to Pas-de-l'Ecluse (or Pas-d'Ecluse), 18¼ (English) miles by the river, is only half that distance in a straight line.

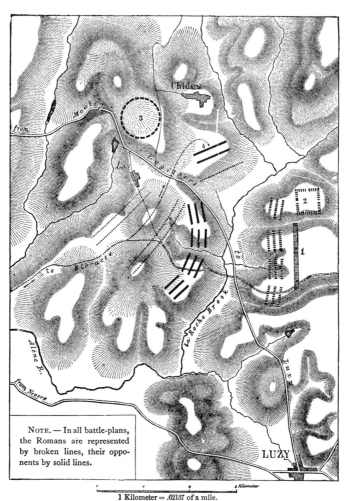

Note. — In all battle-plans, the Romans are represented by broken lines, their opponents by solid lines.

1 Kilometer = .62137 of a mile.

Plan II. *Battle with the Helvetians.* B.G., Bk. I. Chap. 24–26.

1. The new legions and auxiliaries.
2. Cæsar's camp.
3. The Helvetians' baggage, parked.
4. The Boii and Tulingi.

The heavy lines show the first position of the two armies. The mountain to which the Helvetians fled lies immediately west of the modern village of *Las*. Just south of that village, the light dotted lines show the position of the Helvetians at their second attack, and, facing them, the second position of the first two lines of the Romans. The third line has wheeled to the right, to meet the flank attack of the Boii and Tulingi.

112

MAP OF THE
CAMPAIGN OF
B.C. 58.

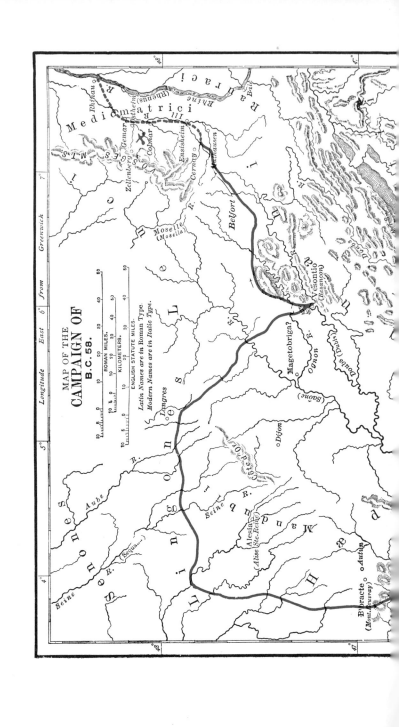

MAP OF THE
CAMPAIGN OF
B.C. 58.

ROMAN MILES.

KILOMETERS.

ENGLISH STATUTE MILES.

Latin Names are in Roman Type.
Modern Names are in Italic Type.

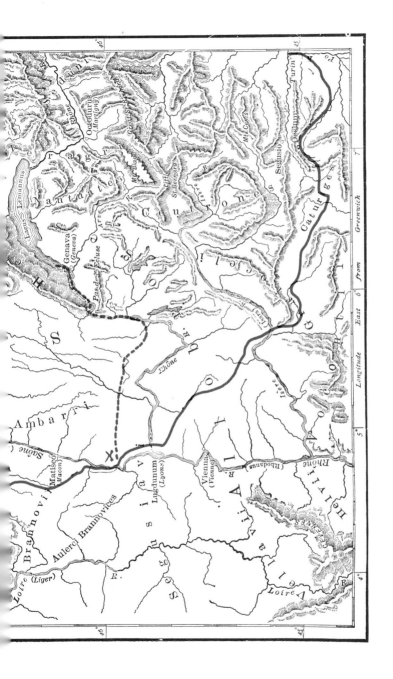

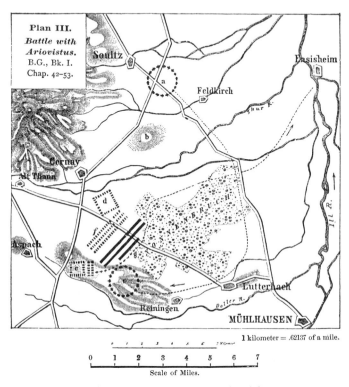

Plan III.

Battle with Ariovistus.

B.G., Bk. I.
Chap. 42-53.

1 kilometer = .62137 of a mile.

Scale of Miles.

a. First camp of Ariovistus.
b. Hill on which the conference was held.
c. Second camp of Ariovistus.
g. German line of battle.
d. Cæsar's larger camp.
e. Cæsar's smaller camp.
f. Roman line of battle.

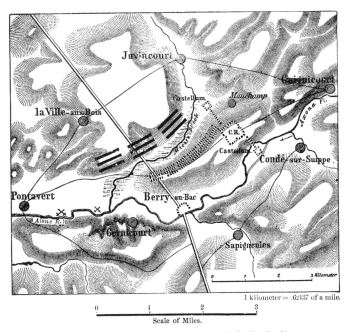

Plan IV. *Battle on the Aisne (Axona).* B.G., Bk. II. Chap. 5-10.

C. R. Castra Romana.

1 kilometer = .62137 of a mile.

Scale of Miles.

MAP OF THE
CAMPAIGN OF
B.C. 57.

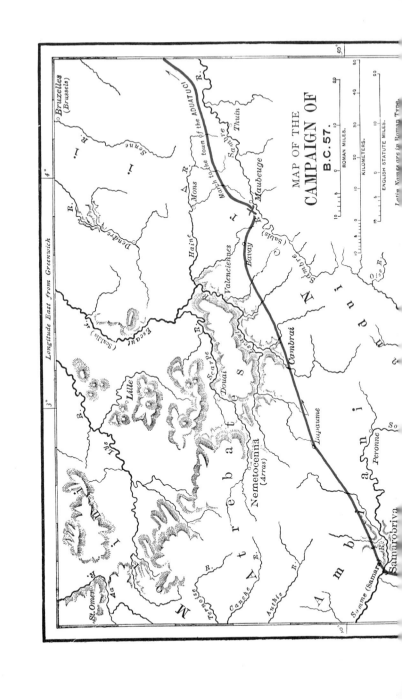

MAP OF THE
CAMPAIGN OF
B.C. 57.

ROMAN MILES.

KILOMETERS.

ENGLISH STATUTE MILES.

Latin Names are in Roman Type.

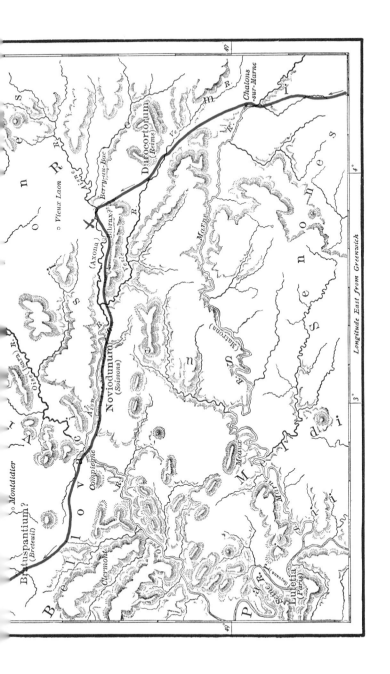

Longitude East from Greenwich

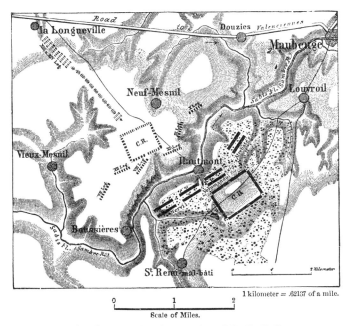

Plan V. *Battle on the Sambre (Sabis).* B.G., Bk. II. Chap. 19–27.

C. R. Castra Romana.   C. B. Castra Belgica.

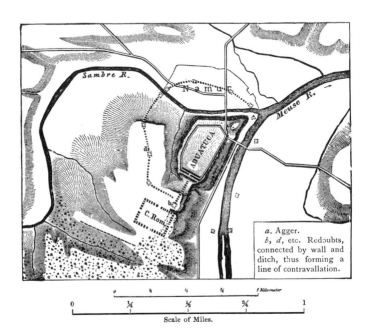

a. Agger.
b, d, etc. Redoubts, connected by wall and ditch, thus forming a line of contravallation.

Scale of Miles.

Plan VI. *Siege of Aduatuca.* B.G., Bk. II. Chap. 29-33.

MAP OF THE
CAMPAIGNS OF
B.C. 55, 54, & 53.

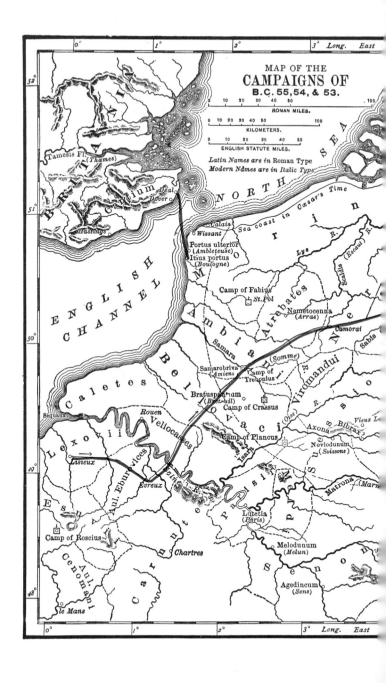

MAP OF THE
CAMPAIGNS OF
B.C. 55, 54, & 53.

Latin Names are in Roman Type
Modern Names are in Italic Type

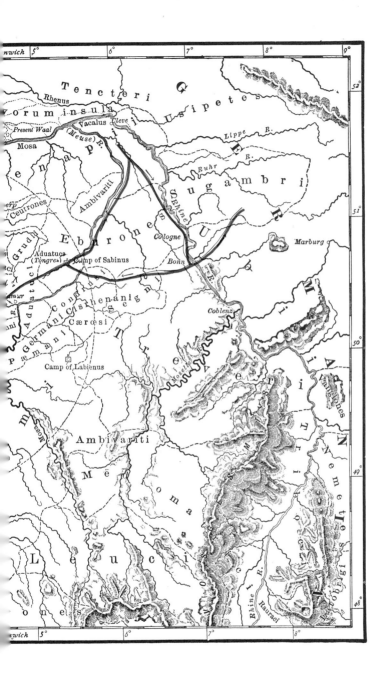

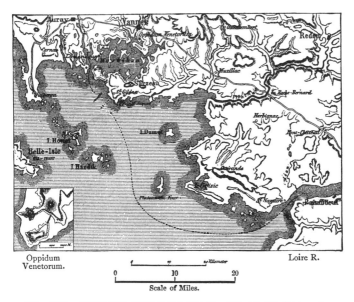

Oppidum
Venetorum.

Loire R.

Scale of Miles.

0   10   20

Plan VII. *Campaign against the Veneti.* B.G., Bk. III. Chap. 7–16.

The dotted line shows the course of the two fleets from the Loire and the Auray
respectively.

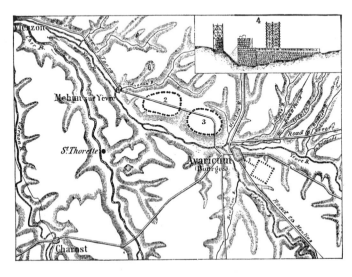

Scale of Miles.

Plan VIII. *Siege of Avaricum.* B.G., Bk. VII. Chap. 23–28.

1. *agger*, pushed towards the town from the Roman camp.
2. First position of Vercingetorix.
3. Second position of Vercingetorix.
4. Section of the *agger*, according to Rüstow.

BRITAIN
IN THE
CAMPAIGNS OF
B.C. 55 & 54.

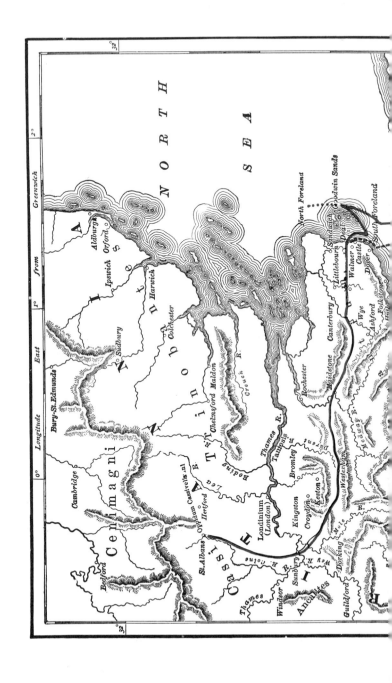

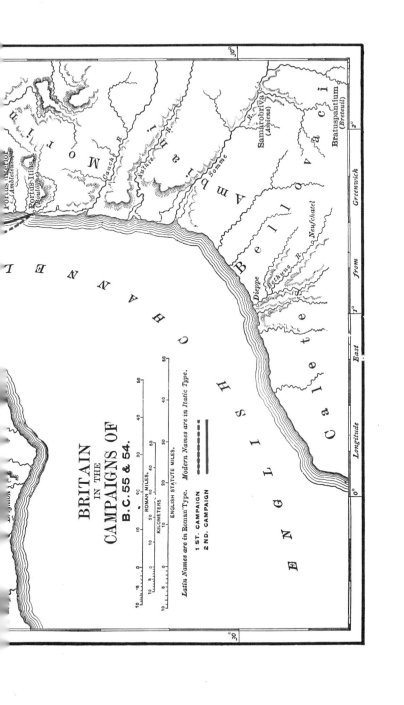

BRITAIN
IN THE
CAMPAIGNS OF
B.C. 55 & 54.

Latin Names are in Roman Type.   Modern Names are in Italic Type.

1 ST. CAMPAIGN
2 ND. CAMPAIGN

ROMAN MILES.
KILOMETERS
ENGLISH STATUTE MILES.

ENGLISH CHANNEL

Calletè

Belloväci

Ambliani

Morïni

Portus Itius
(Boulogne)

Portus Inferior
(Ambleteuse)

Samarobriva
(Amiens)

Bratuspantium
(Breteuil)

Dieppe

Neufchatel

Canche R.

Authie R.

Somme R.

Bethune R.

Longitude   0°   East   1°   from   2°   Greenwich

30°

30°

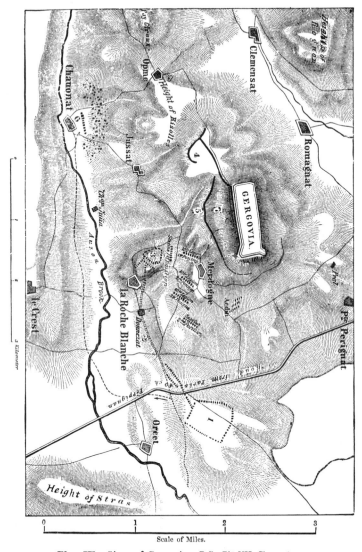

Plan IX. *Siege of Gergovia.* B.G., Bk. VII. Chap. 36–53.

1. Cæsar's large camp.　　2. The double trench connecting the camps.　　3. The small camp.
4. Gallic fortifications.　　5. Gallic wall.　　6. Detached legion.　　7. Gallic camp.

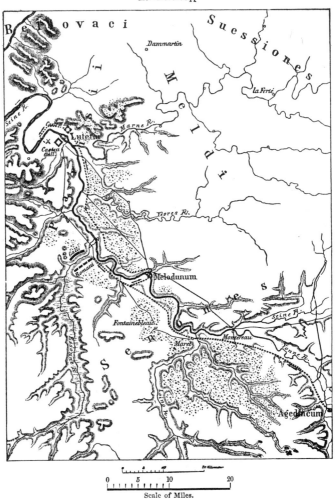

Plan X. *March of Labienus against Lutetia.* B.G., Bk. VII. Chap. 59–62.

MAP CF THE
CAMPAIGN OF
B.C. 52.

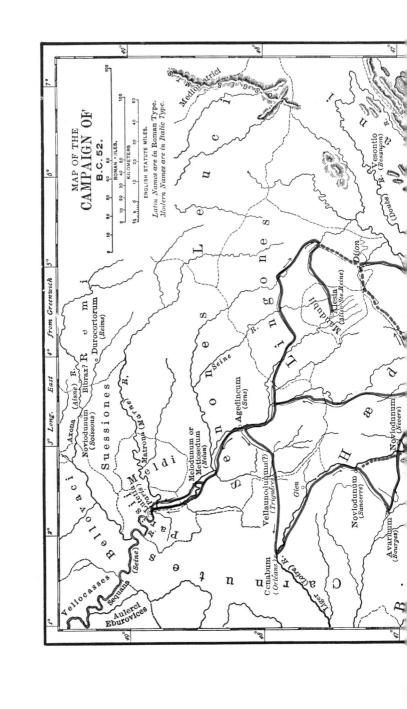

MAP OF THE
CAMPAIGN OF
B.C. 52.

ENGLISH STATUTE MILES.
ROMAN MILES.
KILOMETERS

Latin Names are in Roman Type.
Modern Names are in Italic Type.

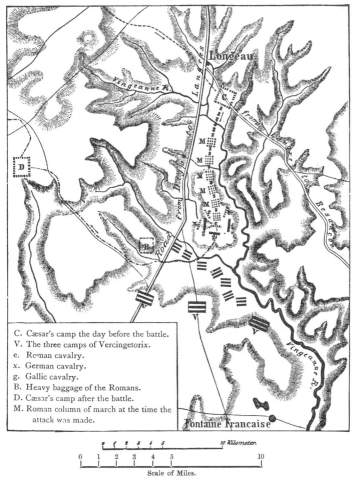

C. Cæsar's camp the day before the battle.
V. The three camps of Vercingetorix.
e. Roman cavalry.
x. German cavalry.
g. Gallic cavalry.
B. Heavy baggage of the Romans.
D. Cæsar's camp after the battle.
M. Roman column of march at the time the attack was made.

Plan XI. *Defeat of Vercingetorix on the Vingeanne.* B.G., Bk. VII. Chap. 66–67.

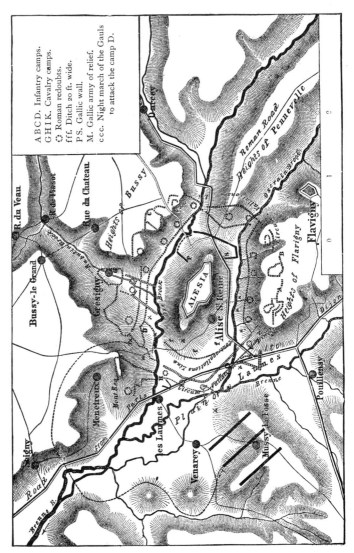

ABCD. Infantry camps.
GHIK. Cavalry camps.
⟳ Roman redoubts.
fff. Ditch 20 ft. wide.
P.S. Gallic wall.
M. Gallic army of relief.
ccc. Night march of the Gauls
to attack the camp D.

Plan XII. *Siege of Alesia.* B.G., Bk. VII. Chap. 68-89.

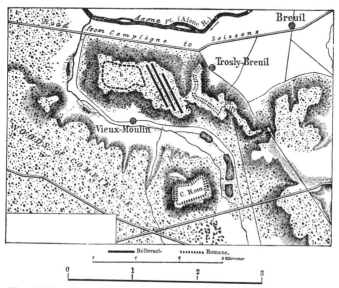

Plan XIII. *Campaign against the Bellovaci.* B.G., Bk. VIII. Ch. 7-16.

C. Rom = Roman camp.
b = Camp of the Bellovaci.
c = Roman army.
d = Army of the Bellovaci.

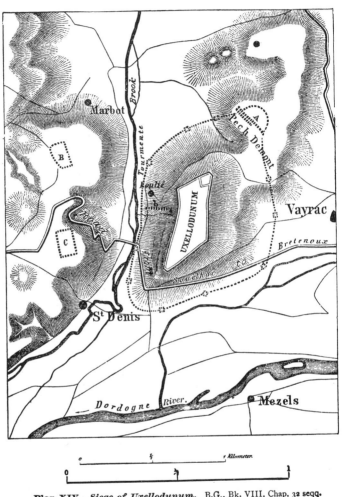

Plan XIV. *Siege of Uxellodunum.* B.G., Bk. VIII. Chap. 32 seqq.

A B C. Roman camps. b. Roman *agger.*

INDEX OF LATIN MILITARY TERMS

INDEX OF LATIN MILITARY TERMS.

Numbers refer to Sections.